MAMA CHIQUITA

Little Mother

by

Felicitas Sistos Saldana

ACKNOWLEDGMENTS

I would like to thank my husband Francisco, for his patience and support during the writing of this book.

To my son Alex for his encouragement and support. He convinced me to continue and finish this project that I had started many years ago.

To my brothers Vito and Angel. To my sisters Rosa, Concha, Nena and Laura for sharing their own experiences in the writings of their stories, which enhance the content of the book and are shared in it.

To Justin, my publisher, whose guidance and support were key to the completion of this project. Special thanks to Maxine for her patience and support. To the rest of the team that assisted me through the long process.

DEDICATIONS

To God, whose presence and light have guided me through the hardships of my life which has not been an easy one.

To my parents Ricardo Sistos and Irene de la Cruz. Especially to my mother, whose vision and courage made it possible for our family to accomplish what seemed impossible: the dream of leaving the original country to get to the land of opportunities.

To the family's relatives who, with their support made the impossible become possible.

To the people who, like angels, surrounded the little mother and little children, who for a while needed to survive by themselves in a strange, unfriendly environment.

CONTENTS

INTRODUCTION

It is always nice to see such a big family get together. This time, we were at Concha's house. She lives the closest to my parents. My father is getting old. He will be 89 years old next May. Who was to say that he was going to live such a long time? He had been a complainer and a very worried person all his life. He turned little issues into big ones. My father was never a social person. As children, we never visit anyone, and no one ever visits us.

Concha and her husband Nazih have a beautiful house, and they are always so willing to have the family over. Concha is a beautiful, very intelligent lady. She was a beautiful baby, the third girl in our family. My mother used to tell us about Lupita, who was born after the first Ricardo. Lupita was only six months old when she died. "Lupita was such a beautiful girl with her beautiful big brown eyes. She looked like your father." I used to imagine how beautiful she must have been. My father was so handsome, and like he used to say, "No one looks like my family. In my family, everyone was good-looking; you all looked like your mother

1

(chatos y feos). Then, Conchita was born, and she was beautiful, not as pretty as Lupita, but she looks like your dad." My mother seemed to be happy. Even my Tia Ofelia, my father's sister, said that she was pretty. Conchita did not have colored eyes. When she was born, my tia Ofelia checked her eyes just like every time my mother had a child. We all waited, hoping that my tia would say, "Yes, the baby has green/blue eyes." the children with fair skin, like Angel, Nena, and Juan, had colored eyes, but they changed before the children turned six months of age. From twelve children, no one had color eyes like my dad's. I now understand how disappointed my mother probably was. She wanted every one of us to look like my father.

When we were little, living in Tijuana, Ricardo, the fourth one in the family, used to say, "I am going to be a doctor when I grow up," and Concha would add, "And I will be your nurse" Sure,,, enough, Ricardo is a doctor, he graduated from Loyola University, and he works for Kaiser Permanente.

Concha is a nurse. She is also the second to the Director of the Los Angeles General Hospital. She also got married and has two beautiful children.

It seems like a dream. The eight children born in Leon Guanajuato, Mexico, became professionals in the United States of America.

Four more children were born in California. They also became professionals with many sacrifices and followed the steps of their older siblings. Lalo was the first one. Then Tere, Laura and Mario also were born in California. Lalo was six months old when the whole family came to California. We managed to live almost six years in Tijuana. When we came from Leon Guanajuato, we did not imagine that it would take us that long to enter the United States of America, the "Land of the Opportunities," but it did.

CHAPTER 1

Today is July 17, 2024. I don't know how many times I've started to write my story. There's something very strong that stops me from continuing. Maybe it's my insecurities and great fears that don't allow me to complete this story— the story of my life. I think I don't believe I'm capable of doing something special and worthy of being read and appreciated. Today, I'm starting again, and this time, I hope I can continue and finish what I have to say. I need to write what I remember on my own, no matter if it's well or poorly written. It doesn't matter if no one ever reads it.

My story is of a family that migrates from their homeland to a new country in search of a better life. It's a collection of the experiences and memories of my parents and brothers/sisters on the journey to get from Mexico to the United States of America. Of all the obstacles and suffering to achieve the American Dream, and how we succeeded!

I am the eldest daughter of Ricardo Sistos and Irene De La Cruz. I was born on December 8, 1945, the day of the Immaculate Conception. I never knew what the time or the day I was born was like. Once, I heard my mom's older brother, named Jesus, mention that the day I was born, he and my dad got very drunk. Ricardo, the fifth child of my parents, was born on the same day five years later. That day, very early in the morning, my dad told me, "You have a new little brother. It's your birthday gift." That's how I've always seen my brother Ricardo as a special gift in my life.

I also knew from a very young age, through my mother, that my dad was expecting a white boy with light eyes like him. But fate had a surprise for him, as I was born a girl with dark skin and small brown eyes. According to my mom, my dad was so disappointed that he didn't even want to see me. I don't know when he finally saw me. I have a feeling that my mom was also disappointed when I was born because her sister, Felicitas, had once told her, when they were young, "If you want to have beautiful children, you have to marry a handsome man." That was one of the reasons she married my dad. But her plan didn't work with me.

There were two other children between Rosalia and me: the first Ricardo, who, according to my mom, was white and had blue eyes. My dad was happy, but little Ricardo died at three months old. Then came Lupita, but she also passed away before her first birthday. From then on, every time a child was born, the first thing they did was check if they were light-skinned and if they had blue eyes. My mom longed with all her heart to give my dad a white child with big, light-colored eyes, handsome like my dad.

My mom had nineteen children, but only twelve of us made it to adulthood. Of the twelve, some were dark-skinned, some were light-skinned, and others were darker, as they used to say, "negrito del mismo arroz," meaning white and dark in the same pot, but none of us had green or blue eyes as my father and my aunt Ofelia (his sister) had hoped. None of the nine children my aunt Ofelia had were born with colored eyes either!

My dad never imagined that the daughter (me) he had so despised for not being what he had expected would become his right hand. "You're taking my right hand," (meaning the one who supported him the most), he told Pancho, my husband, the day he asked for my hand in marriage.

MY FATHER

My father was the son of Angel Sistos Gallardo and Felicitas Barreto Arroyo. We never met them; they both died before my father got married. My grandfather, Angel's parents, were Victorio Sistos and Agripina Arroyo. My father used to say that his father was very intelligent. My grandfather Angel held quite important government positions; he even became the mayor of his hometown, Pueblo Nuevo, Guanajuato, Mexico, the city where my father was also born. Felicitas, my grandmother, was a very fair-skinned woman with beautiful blue eyes. Her last name, Barreto, came from her father, and Arroyo from her mother. It was said that my great-grandfather Barreto was tall and fair, and his wife, my grandmother Felicitas's mother, was short, dark, and had very curly hair. My father said that his mother, apart from being very beautiful, was very kind, almost a saint. As I was the first girl, he wanted to name me Felicitas, a name I never liked. Not only that, but they decided to call me by my grandmother's nickname, (Picha), a nickname I despised, but I was supposed to feel very honored to be the only one among all the descendants of the Sistos Barreto to carry such a name and nickname.

From a very young age, I heard my father say that the members of his family were all very good-looking. He had only one brother named Angel as well, who died very young. My father's sisters were Celestina, the oldest; Tona, a very beautiful woman who never had a family and died young, infected with syphilis by her husband; Concha, who died in childbirth and, according to my father, was a very kind and calm person. She left several very young children when she died. The youngest of my father's family was Ofelia.

On my father's side, I only knew my Aunt Ofelia and my Aunt Celestina, his sisters. The rest of his family had died by the time I was born. Within a span of five years, my father lost his parents, his only brother, and two of his sisters. I understand that when my father was younger, he never drank alcohol, but I believe that after so much loss in his family, he felt very alone and began to drink from then onwards, and it became a habit to drink every eight days, never during the week, but for many years every Saturday he would get drunk and spend all he earned from working.

My Aunt Ofelia lived in Leon, married to Ezequiel; they had nine children, some of whom still live in Leon, Guana-juato. My Aunt Celestina lived in California and married Jose. They also had a very large family. Both my Aunt Celestina and her husband Jose have also passed away, and the rest of their family still live in Burbank, California.

My father was a very nervous man, worried about the smallest problem. This prevented him from being happy and from providing happiness. He loved his country of origin, Mexico. His plan when coming to this country was to work for a while and then return to his land. As the years passed, the family grew, and he never managed to return to his country. From my father, we learned to be proud of our Mexican heritage. To be proud of WHO we are and the great importance of education. He said education is the foundation of success in life.

MY MOTHER

My mother's name is Irene De La Cruz, daughter of Juan De La Cruz and Josefa Hernandez. Her grandparents were Martiniano De La Cruz and Isabel (I don't remember her last name) and Silverio Hernandez and Agripina Romo. I only met my grandmother Josefa, and I vaguely remember my great-grandparents Silverio and Martiniano. From my mother's side, I knew my Aunt Angelita and my Uncle Salvador, the youngest in my mother's family. They lived in La Union De San Antonio, Jalisco, with my great-grandfather Silverio. My grandfather Juan died in the same year I was born. He was a quarry laborer, which was used to build large and beautiful temples and cathedrals. He had an accident while carrying a heavy, carved quarry stone on his back up a ladder. He slipped and fell, and the quarry stone fell on top of him. He probably broke his spine. In his ignorance, my great-grandfather Martiniano, instead of taking him to the hospital, took him to a traditional healer who further injured my grandfather Juan so that after he died, he bled profusely from the mouth.

My Aunt Isabel, we called her Chavela, was the eldest of my mother's family. She lived in Leon, married Cruz, and had a large family with 14 children. We used to visit my Aunt Chavela with my mother almost every eight days. I liked going there because my aunt cooked very tasty food, and there we ate meat and dishes that we didn't have at home. My father didn't come with us; he and my aunt didn't get along because she would reproach him for how badly he behaved towards my mother and us. My Aunt Chavela, as I said, was very good at cooking and also at sewing clothes. She was always very busy making clothes for other people, but her house and her children were always dirty and neglected, the opposite of my mother, who didn't know how to cook—I knew this from a young age because her food had no taste, but we and her house were always clean. When we visited my Aunt Chavela, my mother dressed us in our best clothes and made sure we were very clean, which is why my aunt thought we were in better economic conditions and often reproached my mother, making her cry, yet we continued visiting her, as it was the only place we went to visit. We never visited my Aunt Ofelia, the only sister of my father, because we did not have decent clothing to wear, and we did not have a place in the circle that they moved in. My Aunt Ofelia's family had many wealthy friends; they were not very rich, but they moved in much higher circles, and we were very poor and did not have presentable clothes to socialize with them.

Years later, when we arrived in the United States, I met my aunts Josefina and Felicitas and another brother of my mother named Jesus. My Aunt Felicitas called herself Irene because she took my mother's name when she came to California as a young girl. The reason my Aunt Felicitas changed her name was that when my mother got married, my grandfather Juan allowed her to go to the United States with an aunt who was visiting. He did not want my aunt to marry as young as her sisters Irene and Chavela, who got married at fifteen years old. All three were born in the United States, in different states. My Aunt Chavela was born in Iowa, my Uncle Jesus in Michigan, my mother and Aunt Josefina in California, and Aunt Felicitas in Texas. My grandfather and his family moved continuously from state to state, looking for work opportunities, which is why their children were born in different states of the American Union. When my grandfather Juan looked for the birth certificate of my Aunt Felicitas, he could not find it, and thinking that my mother had already married and might never return to California, he gave her certificate to my Aunt Felicitas. That's why my Aunt Felicitas has been called Irene since then. We never knew in which part of Texas my Aunt Felicitas was born. The last two, my Aunt Angelita and Uncle Salvador were born in Mexico.

My mother was very intelligent but did not have the opportunity to study because when she was of school age, her family was so poor that she didn't have proper clothes or shoes to go to school. She couldn't read. I remember when I did my school homework and asked her about numbers, she would say, "Look at the numbers on the calendar," that's how I learned the numbers.

It's incredible that my mother, who couldn't read in Spanish and didn't know English, when she alone had to come to California, learned how to travel back and forth to Tijuana to see us. She also worked in many places in San Fernando, California. She spent more than five years alone in this country, struggling to support our family in Tijuana. My mother learned to read when Nena, my sister, who was already a teacher, taught her. It was my mother's vision and drive that brought us to this country.

THE MARRIAGE

My father met my mother at a place where they sold juices and ice cream. He began to court her when he was thirty-one, and she was just fifteen. My mother fell in love with my father because he was very handsome, and she believed what her sister Felicitas had told her, "If you want to have beautiful children, marry a handsome man." My mother did not consider herself beautiful. She wanted to have beautiful children, and that was one of the reasons she decided to marry him.

My grandfather Juan realized that my mother was involved with my father and told her, "Irene, that man is not right for you. He is much older than you. He drinks too much and is irresponsible. This will be the last time you see him; go and let him know that you will not see him anymore." Instead of ending the relationship, my mother left with him. My father told her that if they broke up, he would sink deeper into alcoholism. Since she did not want to be responsible for his downfall and was very much in love and proud that a man with so much experience was interested in her, she decided to marry him.

At that time, when a girl left with her boyfriend without being married, she should not live with him until they were married. Since my father's parents had already died and he had nowhere to take her, my father took her to live with his aunt Nicomedes, a cousin of my grandmother Felicitas. My mother stayed there for almost three months as my father struggled to gather enough money to marry her, spending it all at the tavern instead. My grandfather Juan and my father met occasionally, and he demanded that he fulfill his promise to his daughter by marrying her.

Finally, with the help of his sister, Ofelia, my father managed to gather the money needed to marry my mother. They got married on January 29, 1945. My grandfather Juan had to sign to give his consent for their marriage, as my mother was almost a child. He did not allow anyone from his family to attend the wedding, as he never agreed with it and was very hurt by my mother because she disobeyed him on something so important and life-changing. Sister Felicitas went to the mass secretly from her father. It was a very contradictory day for my mother; on one hand, she was very happy to marry the love of her life, but on the other, very sad because her family was not present, especially her father, because she knew that my grandfather Juan loved her very much and she had a beautiful relationship with him, and that day it broke!! My mother was some time without seeing her family. Finally, she went to ask for forgiveness from her father, and he said: "Get up, you don't deserve my forgiveness, I warned you not to marry Ricardo, and you didn't obey me. Your sister Chavela did the same as you, and you saw how badly things went for her. She comes all beaten up every time, and I receive her because she didn't know what she was doing, but you did, I told you, so don't come complaining to me because I won't support you." And so it was. My mother had it worse than her sister and never complained to her father, and she was just a young girl!! My mother asked for his forgiveness several times, and he did not forgive her, allowing her to visit the family, but he was cold and distant with her. On his death-bed, my grandfather Juan could no longer speak, but he looked at each of his children surrounding his deathbed, paused his gaze for a moment on my mother, and with tears in his eyes, he took her hand. My mother cried with joy. Finally, her father had forgiven her, but it was the last time she saw him alive!

OUR LAND

León, Guanajuato is a large city in the center of the Mexican Republic. León is known for being the center of shoe factories in Mexico. It also produces bags, belts, and many other leather goods, some very fine. Of course, my father worked making footwear, specifically finishing shoes.

His job as a shoe finisher was well-paid and respectable. My father was a very good and fast finisher. I believe he made very good money. However, we, his family, could not benefit from his good salary, as he only gave my mother money for the "essentials," meaning she went to the market with very little money. I remember well what my mother brought back when she came from her daily shopping. A quarter liter of milk mixed with corn atole was the food for the youngest child. One or two eggs, a bit of lard, a bit of alphabet pasta or noodles, a tomato, an onion, a few breads, dough for making tortillas, some rice, and beans. Occasionally, she brought some meat and many bones to make beef broth. The vegetables she added to the broth were so few that they didn't even flavor the broth. In the morning, she made the rest of us kids a rice dish, which was supposed to be rice pudding, but it was just rice boiled in water with sugar, and the rice was swimming in the water. What a difference compared to Mrs. Maria, our neighbor, "There goes Doña Maria with her full basket." We sat on the curb, watching skinny Maria, as they disparagingly called her, admiring her large and beautiful grocery basket filled with jellies, candied sweet potatoes, meat, and vegetables for her rich broth; it made our mouths water to see

17

all the good things she had in her basket. "She thinks she's so much because she has a henpecked husband who doesn't go anywhere because he's afraid of his wife, and they even dare to go to mass, even though we all know they're in mortal sin," were the unkind comments from the neighbors. "What a coincidence that they only have four children. Everyone knows they're cheating not to have more kids. Anyone can have a tidy home like theirs who even have a radio, the only ones on the street who have one," was the mentality of most people. Every couple should have ALL the children God sent them. That's what the Catholic priests preached. If a woman confessed to avoiding having a family, the priests excommunicated her for committing an unforgivable sin!!! I, at a young age, didn't understand the comments I heard; to me, those children had a very nice life. The other neighborhood kids and I saw them dressed up and going out together on Sundays. They looked so happy! How was it possible that people like them were in sin? And our parents, who according to them followed God's laws—having all the children God sent them—The "compadres" (friends who get together to drink and call each other compadre) asked each other, how many children do you have? "Seven or eight and still counting," my father would say proudly. It seemed like they were racing to see who could have more children. As if having all the children God gave them was the only commandment they had to obey. And we were tremendously poor. That dark house with just one bedroom and an incredibly low ceiling that leaked every time it rained. There were two beds in the only bedroom. My parents' bed had a mattress. Ours didn't even have that. We all lay across it, and when my feet hung over because I was 'too big,' they laid me on the floor. It wasn't that I was 'too big;' it was that the bed was too narrow. How could my feet not hang off! The little house was small, but we kept it very clean, washing the red brick floor until it shone.

The dirt street in front of our house had to be swept every day. All the neighbors used to do it. I loved to do it. Every day, before the sun came up, every neighbor came out to sweep their part of the street. That was one of my shores that I enjoyed doing because I love to see our whole street so clean.

The reason my father gave so little money to my mother was that every Saturday, he went to the tavern to drink and buy drinks for his friends. "Serve everyone a drink on behalf of Ricardo Sistos" was his motto, and he was very popular for that. Those Saturdays were so sad when I saw my father getting ready, asking my mother for his clean socks and handkerchief. I knew he would go drinking and not return until the next day in the early morning!!

The owner of the factory where my father worked was called Don Octaviano, and he was known as Maestro Octaviano. Knowing his workers, as most of them were irresponsible drunks who neglected their families, thought of protecting the families by lending his workers what they called "el Chivo," or the amount spent on food for the family for a week. On Monday afternoon, Maestro Octaviano met with each of his employees and lent them the Chivo. "Ricardo, how much do you want for your Chivo?" "Give me eighty pesos, maestro," "Only eighty pesos? Is that enough for your wife to feed eight children and you two?" "Oh yes, that's more than enough!" The maestro knew well it was impossible for such a large family to eat the essentials for eighty pesos a week. It would have been good if my mother could have used that money just for food, but from that money, she had to save for the rent and other necessary expenses. The bad thing about all this is that after my father spent the money he kept for his binges if he knew my mother had money saved, he would come back for it. "Please, Ricardo, don't take what I have for the rent. Later we won't have anything to pay it with," "Give me what you have; it's my money, and I do what I want with it. You're no one to tell me what I have to do," These words and others, even uglier, were accompanied by shoving and hits, as my father was very offensive and violent when he drank. My mother ended up giving him all she had. The family kept growing, as a new baby was born each year, but the "chivo" didn't increase, and everything was getting more expensive. That was every week, on Friday, my father paid back what the maestro had lent him on Monday, and the next Monday, the maestro would lend him the "Chivo" again. This way of paying his employees saved many families from going hungry due to the irresponsibility of the fathers, who went to the tavern every eight days to squander their families' livelihood.

Now I know that my mother was very young at that time. I was about seven or eight years old. She would have been only twenty-four or twenty-five. To me, she seemed very old, with straight hair tied in a ponytail at the back of her neck. Her faded dresses, a pair of old shoes that she cleaned every day before putting them on, and a dark, old, faded "rebozo," a shawl that covered her stomach because I always saw her pregnant. Of course, she had a child every year! What a difference when years later she went to live in the United States, and we stayed in Tijuana; she rejuvenated, looked like what she was, a woman in her twenties, very well-kept, she seemed like a different person!! In León, I don't remember her face well, but it was very blotchy. I only remember that she was cold, very cold. I don't remember her giving me a kiss or a hug; she felt so distant, as if she was only physically present. When my mother noticed my presence, it was to scold or hit me for not doing things the way she wanted. From a very young age, I had too many responsibilities. I was a little dark-skinned, short, and very thin girl, and despite that, I had many responsibilities. Whether it was helping to wash clothes, and dishes, sweeping, and going to the store, I had to carry the child who followed the baby, who was very heavy. I studied my summaries and did my school homework at the same time I was washing clothes or dishes. With a child on my back, I would go play with my friends, as that was the only way my mother let me go out to play. Now I understand that the only way my mother could face her life was to become tough and strong, trying not to feel so much mistreatment, but at the same time, she lost her ability to show all her feelings, especially to show us her love and understanding, that's why she was so in-credibly cold, she seemed like a robot that moves and acts without feeling!!

There was a lady near our house in León called Doña Eloisa; she was a very kind person, married to a younger man than her. They said that she had been his teacher. His name was Rufo, and he seemed very serious and always angry, to me at least. My mother washed and ironed clothes for her, and she gave her some money, some fabric cuts, and thread, and my mother made dresses for me and my little sisters. Occasionally, Doña Eloisa asked my mother to let me go to her house to help her with the work. They had four children, two boys and two girls. All were older than me, but they did not help around the house. I liked to help her, although I got nervous when Doña Eloisa sent me for tortillas; I took a long time because there were many people, and the tortilleria staff didn't pay attention to me because I was very small and insignificant. Doña Eloisa also gave me fabric and threads to do the sewing I needed to embroider for my sewing class; it was a requirement that we finish some embroidered garments for the end-of-year classroom exhibition, and the ones I presented were always for other people. I embroidered beautiful pillows, quilts, and other cross-stitch items 'for Doña Eloisa and also for my Aunt Chavela, my mother's sister. I felt proud to be able to embroider such beautiful things, but very sad that I was not able to keep them to enjoy them in our home!!

· THREE KINGS DAY

We Mexicans have many beautiful traditions. One of them is DIA DE LOS SANTOS REYES (Three Kings Day). I have very fond memories of Three Kings Day, on January 6. We looked forward to that day with great anticipation. All year, I tried to behave as best as I could because, depending on that, the Three Wise Men would bring me something from the long list of things I asked for. In the week before January 6, I would write my letter to the Wise Men. I asked for something specific: a doll, a ball, a set of little dishes, and whatever else they wanted to bring me. With much sacrifice, my mother would set aside toys and candies at a store where she paid in installments whenever she could during the year to put them in our shoes on January 6. That day was the most beautiful and awaited day for me. I remember that the night before, I could not sleep from the excitement, but I had to sleep so that the Wise Men would pass by my house. The next morning, we would find a small toy, candies, and peanuts, all beautifully wrapped in cellophane! Early in the morning, very excited, we will get up and go to the "saguan" where the night before, we had lined up our shoes so the Wise Man could leave us our gifts and candies. All the kids on the block came out to show our gifts, and we played all day with our toys. There was one thing I did not understand then; it was supposed that the Wise Men brought us gifts for how well we behaved. I knew some of my friends did not behave very well, yet the Wise Men brought them big, beautiful gifts. We, I thought, "behave as best we can, and our gifts are small." It was something I did not understand, and it did not seem to me that the Wise Men were fair! It was" mi prima Yolanda" (mi cousin) who told me that it was not the Wise Men, but my mother who made sure we always had gifts on Three Kings Day! That was a great sacrifice on her part, and she did not fail to do it every single year we were in Leon. She later told me that the Wise Men never brought her anything and that her older sister told her it was because my mother was bad. She did not want us to feel the way she felt every January 6.

JUAN DE LA CRUZ

My grandfather Juan De la Cruz, was a hardworking man who made significant progress during the time he was in the United States. He was a contractor who hired people to work in the fields. He followed the agricultural seasons, which is why his children were born in different states of the United States. My grandmother Josefa, whom we called Mama Pepa, was a tall, beautiful, dark-skinned woman, and my grandfather Juan loved her very much. Mama Pepa told me about how happy they were when they lived in the United States and how well-off they were economically. But then came the time of the Great Depression, and the United States government began repatriating foreigners, giving them the opportunity to take everything they had and could carry back to their country, with the condition that they never return to the United States. The grandparents returned to Mexico with their five children. They brought with them quite a bit of money they had saved, a large truck, plenty of quality clothing, and some of their furniture.

In Mexico, my grandparents' life changed drastically as Mama Pepa developed epilepsy and my grandfather Juan began spending a lot of money seeking treatment for his beloved wife. He took her to every doctor they recommended, they went to many parts of Mexico, and no one could cure her. Someone told my grandfather Juan that my grandmother Josefa was bewitched. Grandfather took her to many witch doctors who only ended up taking his money. Finally, one witch doctor, who was supposed to be very good, told my grandfather that the person who had bewitched my grandmother had died, and that was why no one could cure her. Mama Pepa believed that a woman who was in love with my grandfather Juan had cast a spell on her. Mama Pepa told me that one morning, she was sweeping the street when the woman who liked my grandfather Juan—who was also a neighbor—offered her tea, and she drank it. She said that when she entered her house, she felt a severe headache so intense that it left her blind. From then on, she was sick and blind every day of her life. She always blamed that woman for all her ailments.

Grandfather Juan had several businesses in La Union De San Antonio, Jalisco, where Mama Pepa's family was originally from. She was the daughter of Silverio Hernandez, a tall, dark-skinned, very romantic man. He was a widower, as Mama Pepa's mother had died several years earlier. I remember him well because when we went to La Union De

San Antonio, he treated us very well. I remember seeing several women with him the times we visited him. I really liked going to the village because my mother let us play outside until very late, and we ate very well. Since my father did not go with us, I felt free and calm without anyone scolding me. Grandfather Juan was not lucky in his businesses in La Union. Later, they moved to Leon, Guanajuato; his family from La Union De San Antonio, Jalisco, also came from there, but my great-grandfather Martiniano lived in Leon. Martiniano De La Cruz was a quarry laborer. At that time, quarry laborers chiseled the quarry stone used to build temples. He worked for a long time sculpting the walls and towers of temples and went blind from not wearing eye protection while chiseling the quarry. Even though grandmother Pepa was so ill, she had five more children in Leon, born in that terrible situation. Only two of the five survived, my aunt Angelita and my uncle Salvador. The others died very young.

Grandfather Juan started other businesses in Leon but spent a lot of time on Mama Pepa's illness. Grandfather Juan began to drink heavily and neglected his businesses even more, and the employees stole from him. Not only that, but he also neglected the family; friends and relatives who came to visit also stole many things that they had brought from the United States to the extent that the De La Cruz family ended up completely poor. They were so poor that the little children would go from house to house among the neighbors, asking for a taco to eat. What a difference from the full life they had in the United States!! Mama Pepa, crying, remembered the pots of food she threw away because they had plenty of everything. It was despairing for her that in the moments of lucidity she had, she realized that her children were crying from hunger and cold, and she could do nothing to help them. She had very strong and frequent epileptic attacks; sometimes, she would fall on the coals of the stove where she was cooking and burn all over. Many times after an attack, she would be like crazy for a few hours and also was blind.

Desperate to see how much poverty his family was enduring, Grandfather Juan went north with the hope of crossing to "the Other Side." For several months, the family heard nothing from him. The day he returned, dirty and hungry and poorer than ever, he found my grandmother very ill, all burned and battered from so many falls, as there was no one to take care of her. Not only that, he found the youngest girl named Juanita lying down. They didn't know

29

what had happened; my mother was very young then and doesn't remember what happened, but the girl was dead. My mother remembers that her father embraced all his children and cried out loud. Later, my mother learned that her father had been in jail. How many times did Grandfather Juan try to cross to the United States, and how many times he was caught and sent back to Mexico? Grandfather did not want to return to his family defeated and kept trying to cross until he was put in jail. Of the children born in Mexico, only two survived; the others died very young.

ANGEL SISTOS

My father grew up in a very different environment from my mother. His family was never wealthy, but they lived like the wealthy most of the time. My grandfather Angel was very educated and always worked in office jobs. When he wasn't working in the government palace, he worked in a parish office, and he even became the mayor of his hometown, Pueblo Nuevo, Guanajuato, where he was born. For this reason, my grandfather Angel did not like living in the United States, as he was not accustomed to physical labor, which he had to undertake there. My father inherited his love for poetry and acting from his father; I believe that if my father had the opportunity, he would have pursued a career in the arts. He told us that he participated in some theater plays. My father enjoyed reciting poetry and singing. He also wrote down his thoughts, and he wrote a beautiful poem for each of his children. I think my father lived with a lot of frustration for not having done in life what he liked, which could be one of the reasons why he drank so much wine, as he apparently was never happy. Now, I know that my father could have suffered from very serious depression, but at that time, emotional or mental illnesses were not recognized. If someone had a mental or emotional illness, it was denied and considered a shame. I remember hearing many times, "You see how your father is, very nervous, very angry," because of that, my siblings and I learned from a very young age not to make noise, not to upset my father. We became invisible, and all our efforts were to please my father, although we never succeeded! It was incredible that a family of twelve children plus the parents, by six in the evening, which was when my father went to bed, we would all be quiet in our rooms, which were three: one for the six girls, another for the six boys, and the third for my parents. And the rooms were not very big! Of course, that house in Pacoima was large compared to the little room where we lived in Tijuana, and for us to have been able to buy that new house, which I thought was beautiful, was one of our first achievements in this New Land of Opportunities!! We also learned not to give our parents any problems. Each of us tried to solve any problem and helped each other. Like when Angel was at fault in a car crash he had with a lady, and I helped him pay the cost, and our parents never knew about it. On another occasion, Vito got a ticket for crossing a street where he shouldn't have. He was walking! We had to go to court, and the judge forgave the infraction. Our parents knew nothing about that either. We, the children, hid from them what we thought would bother them!

My grandmother Felisa and the rest of the family did like life in the United States. My father did not talk much about that time because, like his father, he also did not like living there. One of the reasons was that he was very patriotic and did not want to salute the Flag of the United States because it was not his flag. That's why he arrived late to school after the pledge of allegiance had passed. He also learned English reluctantly. All his siblings spoke English well, and he only knew the essentials. Grandfather Angel did not like fieldwork. But, since he did not speak English, he could not find work in what he was accustomed to, office work, and had to work in the fields; that's why he did not like life in the United States of America. My father talked a lot about a place near Santa Barbara, California, called La Limonera, where he lived with his family. His brothers, who were older than him, were very popular there; several families invited them to their parties, and they sang and cheered them up!

SISTOS FAMILY

The Sistos family also returned to Mexico around the same time as the De La Cruz family. My father was about 15 years old at the time. Initially, they went to Pueblo Nuevo, and since they brought their money with them, they set up a candle factory. They also made chocolate and candies and had a well-stocked store. The family had plenty of everything and lived comfortably and very peacefully, as Pueblo Nuevo was a small but very picturesque and beautiful city. On Sundays, they were given spending money which they could spend on whatever they wanted. Those years were the happiest for my father. My father had four sisters and one brother. Celestina, the oldest, stayed in the United States because she was already married when the Sistos family returned to Mexico. The family took the first daughter of my uncle Jose and aunt Celestina to Mexico, as my aunt was about to give birth to her second child. They thought that after the birth, they would also go to the city of Pueblo Nuevo in Guanajuato, but they never did, and they had many children after Lola, the first, and never returned to Mexico. Tona and Concha were older than my father. Angel was the only brother; he was a very handsome boy and liked to sing. My father told us that my aunt Tona and uncle Angel formed a duo and, according to my father, sang beautifully at family parties, especially when they were in the United States, as the family was very popular and very happy at that time. My aunt Concha also got married in the United States to Marcelino and already married and pregnant, she went to Mexico with her family. Her children were born in Mexico. She died in childbirth, also very young, and left her very young children orphaned; they suffered a lot as children, but the oldest, my cousin Daniel, went to the United States and worked hard, but he managed to support all his siblings.

My uncle Angel did not end well, as he married a girl with a bad reputation who deceived him, and because of that, they separated; he took to drinking and disappeared for a long time until someone found him in Mexico City, like

34

a beggar, and brought him back to Leon. My uncle Angel ended up getting very sick with a severe liver disease and died very young at my parents' house. My mother cared for him a lot, as he was good to her and defended her from my father when he came home drunk and mistreated her. My uncle Angel had two children, the only ones besides my father's sons who carried the Sistos surname. Their names were Rodolfo and Ruben. My father was very shy all his life. When he was a boy, his sister Tona tried to help him overcome his shyness. My aunt was the complete opposite. Nothing was difficult for her. Without knowing anyone, she went to Las Fabricas de Francia, a very important clothing store in Leon, and asked for clothes on credit so that my father could sell clothes on installment in the rancherias near Leon. But even that did not help my father lose his shyness. Apparently, none of my father's brothers or sisters were as shy and nervous as my father.

Tona married a very wealthy man in Mexico who had syphilis and infected her. No one knew this at first. My aunt got pregnant several times but lost her babies, and they didn't know why until she started to get very sick and was diagnosed with syphilis. She suffered a lot and died very young. My father remembered his sister Tona fondly, as she

35

always tried to help him overcome his shyness and be more sociable. My aunt Antonia wanted my father to be a successful merchant who overcame his fears. But she did not succeed, as fear and being unsociable dominated my father all his life. The only way he overcame them was by drinking a lot of wine. I think that was another reason why he did it. My father and my aunt Ofelia were orphaned very young. My aunt married Ezequiel and took Lola, her niece, to live with her, and my father went to live with some relatives. I know my grandmother Felicitas died of cancer, and I don't remember my father mentioning how my grandfather Angel died.

ONCE MARRIED

Initially, my parents moved close to my mom's parents. It was a very bad decision, as my dad and my grandfather Juan did not get along. When my dad drank, he became very violent and almost always looked for a fight. My dad insulted my grandfather Juan a lot when he was drunk. Several times, my grandfather Juan pretended to be deaf and did not leave his house when my dad insulted him. Until one day, my grandfather could no longer tolerate the insults and confronted my dad with a machete in hand. My poor mother, heavily pregnant, stood between them and pleaded with my grandfather: "Please, Dad, don't fight with my husband. He's very drunk and can't even defend himself, do it for me." My dad was so drunk that he could barely stand, but he kept insulting my grandfather. With tears in his eyes, my grandfather Juan told my mom: "For you, only for you, I won't give Ricardo what he deserves," and went back into his house while my dad yelled, "Coward, damn Lomo Largo, why don't you come out?" People from Guanajuato did not like those from Jalisco who came looking for fortune in León, as some arrived very poor and in a short time, through hard work and sacrifices, managed to own their businesses. That's why they disdainfully called them "lomo largos" because the people from Jalisco were generally quite tall. Many times, I heard my mom say, "If only your dad were like mine, who when he drinks doesn't bother anyone, just comes home to sleep, but your dad always comes home looking for trouble and doesn't let us sleep all night."

CHAPTER 2

When my father found out that my mother was pregnant again, he had a fit. He did not want any more children, and yet he did not want my mother to use contraceptives because, as a Catholic, that would have been a mortal sin. I confronted him. Very seldom would I be able to express my feelings to anyone, and I was very afraid of him, but that time I was so angry that I exploded. "Do you think it is only my mother's fault?" You are the father; you are also responsible." He was going to hit me for saying that to him, but I did not care. My mother and I had kept the secret for a while. I had taken my mother to the doctor, and she was a few months pregnant when we had to tell him.

My father had been complaining of an ulcer. He wanted to go to León to have surgery. It was too expensive to have it in California. We were born in Leon Guanajuato, and one of my tias and her family were there. The actual reason for my father to go to Leon was to be with them. He loved his sister very much and had not seen her in years. He went to Leon. He did not take into consideration our financial problems. At this point, we had bought a house and were having economic problems. It was the worst time to be spending money traveling. He had told my mother that he was already bleeding and that he had to have the ulcer removed. He spent some time with his sister in Leon and came back. He did not have the surgery; he said that he was told that he did not need it. He spent all the money that he took with him. A few months later, a beautiful, sweet little girl was born. She was named Teresa. I took my mother to the hospital where she was born. Tere was the third child born in the United States of America. My mother had a very hard time when she was expecting Teresa. Due to that fact, she resented that new little girl and was very cold to her and mistreated her for many years. Tere remembers that when she was about four or five years old, she used to think, "This lady is not my mother. She hates me," and every day in the afternoon, she would sit outside on the stairs to wait for her mom to come and pick her up, sadly, she would realize once more, "She did not come again. Maybe she will come tomorrow."

During the time that my mother was in California and my father and I were in Tijuana, a girl was born in California. My mother named her Gloria Guadalupe. She was named after a lady that my mom met during her pregnancy and also after the first Guadalupe, who had died as a baby. My mother had been staying with some of my father's relatives. She would be going from one house to another and end up living with her new friend, Gloria. Gloria and her family supported my mom until Gloria Guadalupe was born. This family wanted to adopt my sister, Gloria. My mother needed to work, and she did not have anyone to take care of her little girl. My mother consulted my father about the adoption, and he said: "We will never give one of our children away, bring her to Tijuana, and we will take care of her." Up to then, I had taken care of all the children with very little help from my dad. Juanito, the youngest, was only six months old, and Vick was one year and a half old. Juanito was sick to his stomach almost every day. I was only twelve years old then, a child taking care of seven children. My mom brought Lupita to us, she was about two months old. A beautiful child with black curly hair and big dark eyes. I took care of her the best I could, but she began to be sick to her stomach. My father and I took her to the doctor, and he tried to give her treatment, but Lupita was already too weak and did not respond to the treatment. She was used to another way of living and could not survive the bad living conditions that our family was in. My dad informed my mom about Lupita being very sick, and my mom came to take her back to California to seek medical help. While going back on the bus, my mom noticed that Lupita was not moving. She got off the bus and went back to Tijuana with her dead child in her arms!! This was not all, when she got to the house, almost in the morning, my father was not in. Like other times, he accompanied my mother to take the bus to California and went to the bars to spend the little money that my mom had given him. My mother could not believe that he was capable of doing something like it.

Life had not been easy. Coming to Tijuana took a lot of courage. It was my mother who initiated the move. It is unbelievable that a woman who was so afraid of her husband was able to convince him to move. He had never even changed jobs because he was afraid of changes! The decision was made, but there was no money for the trip. A letter was sent to my father's cousin and sister in California, asking them for help. My father's sister made a collection between her children, and my father's cousin collected from his brothers and sisters. My tia sent us one hundred dollars to cost the trip. My parents sold whatever they could; we did not have much, and most of our furniture was very old. We began our new adventure, not knowing what to expect.

Leon is a big city. It is known for making some of the best quality shoes in Mexico. My father had a good job and made decent money, but his children did not benefit from that. He would spend much of the money drinking every weekend. My father was not a bad person, but because of his drinking, he was not able to provide for his family a decent living. We were in need of the most essentials. My mother was too afraid to complain or to say anything to him. Everyone was terrified to see him drunk. When he was sober, he was not very pleasant. He would not speak to us;

42

he seemed to be always angry, but he was not violent. When he drank, the story changed. He would become very violent. He would fight with the neighbors. If any of his children did something that he did not like during the week, he would not say anything, but when he came back from his "parrandas," you better be ready to have it!

My mother and I, the oldest child, would make sure to be behind the door when we heard him coming. We would know because he would be shouting very loud, so everyone could be heard, "Here I come. If you do not like it, come out and let me know." Of course, the neighbors knew better not to come out. Everyone knew that he had had terrible fights with his neighbors some years before. If my mother would not open the door at the first knock, he would yell, "Where were you? Who was with you? "

He was very annoying when he was drunk; he would want my mother and me to stay up the whole night listening to his conversations that, most of the time, made no sense, and we had to agree to everything he said anyway. That was in the best of the cases.

Sometimes, he would come and ask his wife for the money she had saved to pay the rent at the end of the month. She had to give him the money, or else he would abuse her. He would take the money and would go back to continue his "parrandas" until he spent all the money with his friends. The following day my mother would have to borrow a few pesos to buy beans, masa, one egg, and one quarter of milk to make the baby's "atole" half milk and half water with "maiz." That is what her children would eat. Flouting beans (more water than beans), egg with salsa, one egg, a lot of water, a little tomato sauce, and a few tortillas.

There was a family next door where the father did not drink. It was unusual because all the other fathers did drink, some more than others. This mother was the only one who would buy all kinds of goodies for her children. Every one of us would wait outside to see the mother coming with her beautiful "canasta" with plenty of fruits, vegetables, bread, cakes, and many other wonderful things that the children of the other families would never taste. This family had the luxury of a radio. All the neighbors were able to listen to the music and the stories.

But this couple was not welcome by the neighbors because, according to them, they were breaking the promise they made when they got married and agreed to have all the children that God would send to them. So, they were committing a mortal sin. I was a very small child then, but I

44

could not understand how this couple was in mortal sin when their four children looked so happy and well off. That was the influence the Catholic Church had on the community. People believed that they needed to follow every rule of their religion. What is hard to believe is that as long as they had many children, which they did, they were good people, even if they mistreated and neglected them.

The firstborn Ricardito, was also a beautiful baby, according to my mother. He might have had blue eyes, and he probably would have looked like my father. I was the firstborn to my mother. My father was expecting that my mother was going to have a blond, blue eyes boy. What a surprise!! I was not a boy. I was a small, skinny, dark, not-pretty girl. My father did not even want to see me. I can imagine how disappointed my mother felt. One of the reasons that she married my father was because she wanted to have beautiful children; that was what her sister told her. "If you marry a handsome man, your children will be pretty." So, when I used to hear that Ricardito and The first Lupita were so beautiful and looked like my father and died, my thoughts were, "Why do beautiful people die and ugly people like me live?." Before Angel, Rosalia was born. I did not know if she was pretty or not. What I remember my parents saying was that she was a fat little girl. My father called her "canica." My mother was very careful with Rosa because Ricardito died of Pneumonia, and Lupita died of diarrhea. My parents even bought special milk for her. They probably felt responsible for their two children's dead. Angel was the baby born after Rosa; he was a blond big boy. People used to say that he looked like a German boy. I was confused then, if Angel was so blond and he looked like a German, why was he not considered a beautiful kid by my parents? Angel was named after my paternal grandfather. My father named most of his children after his parents, brothers, and sisters.

The second Ricardo was born the day that I turned five years old. When my mother was going to have a child, we were sent to the park during the day. The day that Ricardo was born, we were taken to the park. When we came back, my father told me, "I have a surprise for you. You have another brother, and he is your birthday present because he was born on your birthday." My new brother was small and dark like me, but his features were delicate like my dad's. After the second Ricardo, my mother had another boy who was born prematurely. He was named Juan Diego. My mother wanted to name someone after her father's name.

My father did not want to because he despised my mother's family, but he agreed to name this child Juan Diego, and we called him Dieguito. Diego was not able to breathe and needed tanks of oxygen. My parents were able to buy only one tank. Dieguito died from lack of oxygen.

Then another girl was born, she was named Concepcion, she had big beautiful eyes and curly hair, still no blue eyes, another disappointment for my father and his sister Ofelia. This little girl would become a beautiful, very smart young girl. My father was then very pleased to have her as his daughter.

One more girl came into our family. This time, my father named her Irene, like my mother. This little girl was "muy Guera" (blonde), at least, my father said: "Another one, no blue eyes." She was not what he really wanted, but at least she was not "prieta" (dark skin). She was beautiful, a thought, with her big brown eyes. Although no color eyes. Actually, the color eyes came from my grandmother, my father's side of the family. Since my mother's side of the family had no color eyes, there was no possibility that we could inherit the color eyes. If my father and tia would have known that, they would have stopped expecting the colored

47

eyes every time a child was born. I realized now how sad my mother was not being able to please my father.

In Leon, we lived in a home with one bedroom and a small kitchen in front of it. When my mom's labor began, we needed to be as far as possible. She had all her children at home, no doctor, no nurse, just a lady who would help her through the process. After Irene, who we call Nena, a boy was born. He was named Victorio, like my dad's grandfather. We call him Vito. He was born in the middle of the night. My father woke us up and took us to the kitchen. Other times, we would be taken to the park, and we had to stay there until the child was born. This time, we could not go to the park, so we were moved to the kitchen. The kitchen was very small, so we laid down on the floor with our heads out of the kitchen. We heard my mom cry and then the cry of a baby; at that time, as we were looking at the sky, we saw a falling star. We always thought that Vito was very special, because of this event. He was very wise and smart at a very young age and continues to be a very special brother.

The last child born in Leon was a boy, he was named Juan Ignacio. My father named most of his children after the names of the members of his family. My mother wanted to name the last child Juan, after her father. My father agreed, but he was also named Ignacio, and we were to call him "Nachito," not Juan. He also had white skin and blond hair. His eyes were checked, and they were blue! Everyone was happy. Although my father's comment was, "I hope the eyes won't change this time," Juanito's eyes changed when he turned six months of age. One more disappointment for my father and another sad moment for my mother, who cannot please my father.

CHAPTER 3

GOOD MEMORIES

Every morning before going on errands, my mom would give us a little cup of Yerba Buena tea. As soon as we woke up, we all shouted, "Water, water," loving how delicious that warm tea tasted in the morning! Sometimes, I stayed behind to watch the rice that my mom left cooking; occasionally, it would spill over, and other times, it would burn because the stove flame couldn't be controlled. The rice, which was supposed to be rice pudding, had very little rice and no milk because the half liter of milk that my mom could buy was mixed with white atole and was the food for the child following the baby, whom my mom could no longer feed as she already had a new baby. My mom had a child every year, sometimes even sooner. As soon as she was out of quarantine, she was pregnant again. When we moved from Leon to Tijuana, we were eight children, and that was because a few had already died. After Vito, Juan Ignacio was born, the last of the Eight born in Mexico. He was also very fair with colored eyes, but before he was six months old, they changed. He still has light eyes, but they are not blue or green as my dad and mom wanted. Colored eyes appeared in some of the grandchildren and great-grandchildren of my parents, finally!!

When we lived in Leon, I remember that after dinner, my mom would sit at the door for a while to chat with the neighbors, as was the custom; many moms did this, and we would play with the children who lived nearby. Usually, they were younger children, including all my little siblings. I didn't have friends my age, as my mom wouldn't let me go out without my siblings. But I loved playing with the younger kids' games like "La Vivora de La Mar," "Los Encantados," and many others. Also, my mom would tell us many stories about princesses and enchanted places. My mom couldn't read, as she never went to school, but my grandfather Juan, her dad, had a book of stories called "The Thousand and One Nights," and he read the stories to his children, and my mom memorized some of them. I remember how I imagined the beautiful princesses with their dresses, one the color of the Wind, another the color of the Moon, and a third the color of the Sun. Not only that, the dresses were so fine that when storing them, the princesses would put one in an orange, another in a walnut, and the last in a pine nut. In those enchanted places where the princesses lived, who were also extremely beautiful, everything was possible, what you desired you had without any problem, where everyone was happy, immensely happy! During the day, I would hurry to finish the house chores and schoolwork with the hope that my mom would continue the story that she had left off the previous afternoon because when my dad came home from work, everything ended, and it was time to sleep, no matter that the rest of the kids continued playing outside. When my dad was at home, everything was silent, as he was bothered by the noise. It was always like this. It was incredible that in a house where there were so many children and later teenagers and adults, when we grew up, by the time he went to bed, almost at dusk, everything was silent, the TV was turned off, everyone to their bedrooms, when we were better off and could have three bedrooms, one for my dad and mom, another for the six girls, and another for the six boys. That was already in the United States. But it was always like that in Leon and also in Tijuana. Although for a while, during the more than five years that we were in Tijuana, both my dad and mom went to work in California, we, the eight who came from Leon, stayed alone. That was our best time, as we were very responsible, and everyone fulfilled their obligations, but we also gave ourselves time to listen to music, watch television, and even dance! Some of my older siblings remember that time with joy and as one of the best times! Later, still in Leon, we moved to another new house that had only two rooms, one of which was the kitchen. That house was built on a very large lot; instead of a yard, it had a huge hole; they said it had been a cemetery for a time. When we moved there, it was a dump, which we completely cleaned, and my dad planted many pumpkins and corn. After a while, everything looked quite nice. My dad had a very special gift. Everything he planted grew and flourished. His grandfather Victorio taught him to till the land and plant vegetables and fruits. My dad remembered his grandfather Victorio fondly; they said that my dad resembled him a lot, even in his sternness. As I already said, my dad's dad was named Angel Sistos, and my dad told us he was very intelligent and educated. He held government positions in his hometown, Pueblo Nuevo Guanajuato, even becoming the town president. Also, the Sistos family lived for a time in Leon after they came from the United States.

HARD TIMES

I attended the government school called Josefa Ortiz de Dominguez, an all-girls school. I remember my school fondly; I was very happy there, loved studying, and always had top grades in my class. I suffered a lot when my mom wouldn't let me go to school because I had to help take care of my siblings when she had errands to run. I also didn't have time to study and would study while washing dishes or the children's clothes, or with a one-year-old child in my arms. I longed to go to my friend Laura's house to embroider my sewing. But my mom rarely let me go, as there was always so much work at home. My friend Laura's life was very different from mine. She only had one older sister and two younger brothers. Laura's only responsibility was to go to school and do her homework. I envied her for that, but even so, I had better grades than her. My notes were impeccable, and everything was in order. We didn't have books for different subjects, just a reading book. We had two notebooks that we divided into sections for each subject and the teacher would write a summary for each subject on the blackboard, and we would copy it into our notebooks. My notes were always up to date. Some of my classmates copied my work; I let them copy it in exchange for them buying me popsicles and milk jellies. In the classroom, I usually sat on the front bench because I couldn't see the blackboard. Sitting next to me were Ofelia and Luisa, the most quarrelsome and tough girls in the class. I let them copy my work, and during exam time, I gave them the correct answers, under the condition that they choose me to play sports during recess, as they were the team captains and I was terrible at sports, but they had no choice but to pick me or I wouldn't let them copy.

I also had another great friend named Ana; she was poorer than me and also smarter. She lived on the outskirts of Leon and walked a long distance to attend school. I really cared for Anita, but Laura looked down on her because she was poor. School was my escape, as my life was very difficult, filled with fear of both my dad and my mom. I never wanted to miss class, but often had to, as my mom needed me to stay home to take care of my little siblings. I cried a lot when that happened.

My dad was very stern. During the week, he didn't talk much, but his mere presence instilled fear in me. But nothing compared to Saturdays, when I would see him get dressed and angry at my mom because his socks and his handkerchief weren't ready when he asked for them. I knew he was going to the bar and wouldn't return until early Sunday morning. "Here comes Ricardo Sistos, and where he draws the line, no one crosses it," were the shouts that woke me up and made me tremble with terror. "Mom, Dad's coming home drunk. What anguish! I feel a hole in my stomach as if my heart wants to jump out." My mom and I would wait behind the door, shivering from the cold and fear, fear? No, it was terror! – "Why won't you open? Who were you with?" "With no one, Ricardo, I fell asleep, I was waiting for you, and you didn't come." – "You have to wait for me no matter what time I get here. Don't you like it when I come home? No, Ricardo, I'm not mad, I'm glad you came home." "I don't even know why I come home, if it weren't for my children, I wouldn't be with you. You're good for nothing. I've never loved you." That's how the rest of the night would go, my dad ranting about nonsensical things, not letting us sleep. Other times, my dad would come home looking to fight with the neighbors, and if no one responded because they already knew him, he would kick their doors. This happened with his "compadre," Domingo (he had baptized my brother Angel), who lived next door to us. I remember the

MAMA CHIQUITA: LITTLE MOTHER

day when the compadre came out and responded. They started to fight, but my dad was so drunk he couldn't land a punch on the compadre. The compadre was sober; he didn't drink, which is why my dad didn't like him, calling him henpecked. "Run Picha" – that's what they called me because they named me Felicitas like my dad's mom, and they called me Picha. My Aunt Ofelia told my dad, "Her name is Felicitas, and we'll call her Picha like my mom." – "Go get your Aunt Ofelia to control your dad. She's the only one he listens to." How far is my Aunt Ofelia's house? Which way do I have to go? No, it's not this way, I already passed by the Barrio, and I can't remember which streets I have to take. I need to go back to the Park, I always go by the Park, why did I come through the Barrio? I was only seven or eight years old then. So much responsibility at such an early age. How many anguishes each time my dad came home drunk. "I think it's this way, I remember I have to pass the park and follow the main street. I don't like passing through this ugly and lonely alley. It scares me! I knew it depended on me for my Aunt Ofelia to arrive in time to stop the terrible fight, so I ran desperately. "Oh God, help me arrive on time!" But I got lost and had to return and take the path that led to the Park and from the Park to the house where my Aunt

Ofelia lived. Oh no! There's a group of people in front of my house. They must be watching my dad's fight. I can't stop. I have to hurry and get to my Aunt's house.

"Tia, (Aunt) Ofelia, please come with me. My dad is having a very ugly fight with the neighbor, Angel's Godfather. Let's go, daughter, hurry." What happened, Daughter? Why did it take you so long? It's because I went through the Barrio and got lost and had to return to the park and finally found my Tia's house." Where's Ricardo? my Tia asked, "He's washing his face. If you had seen Ofelia, what an ugly fight. Godfather Domingo hit him a lot! Ricardo was so drunk he could barely stand, trying to pick up stones to defend himself and couldn't." Ricardo looked like a Holy Christ, all bloodied. But he started the fight, went and shouted many ugly things at the godfather. When he didn't respond, he kicked the door, then the godfather came out and even bit Ricardo on the face."

"Hello, Hermanita (Little Sister)" – Don't talk to me, you shameless man, you're back at it, why don't you understand? Don't you feel ashamed of these children? Look how scared they are. Look at your youngest daughter so pretty, my Conchita. Do it for her, Little Brother. Stop drinking. You go crazy when you do it. Yes, Little Sister, forgive me, you're right! I won't do it again." My Tia Ofelia was holding Conchita; she was born almost three years after Ricardo. Before her, a boy named Juan Diego was born, but he died because he was born prematurely, and my parents only had money for an oxygen tank, and he needed more. Conchita was and is a very beautiful girl, she had fine features and beautiful big brown eyes, and her curly hair like my dad and like Ricardo, my brother. I think they are the ones who most resemble my dad.

My dad was so gentle with his beloved Little Sister. He only obeyed her. No matter how drunk he was, even though she was younger than him, he respected her greatly. To me, what my dad said were just words, how many times I heard the same promises "Now yes, little old lady, I promise I will never drink again." I don't know if my mom believed him, but she was so obedient that on Sunday, when my dad woke up very sick from the "Hangover," she gave him his teas with alcohol and took care of him all day so that he would wake up well another day and my dad could go to work, because that yes, he never missed a day of work, for that he was very responsible. So, another week passed, and the next Saturday, he paid the boss what he had borrowed for the Chivo "Goat" and again went to the bar to spend all the money he had left on wine for himself and his buddies "Serve everyone on behalf of Ricardo Sistos." That time, my dad had such an ugly fight that all my siblings witnessed the fight. Ricardo, my brother, must have been about three years old and got so scared that he fell ill with a disease that turned him Yellow, and he lost a lot of weight. He was like this for a long time until my dad donated a blood transfusion, and finally, he recovered his health. My mom did everything possible for us to move house, as she was very afraid that my dad would fight again with godfather Domingo. The house where we had lived until then had a corridor where there was a wooden bench that had belonged to my dad's mom. The little house had only one bedroom with a very low ceiling, and when it rained, all the water came in because the roof was very bad. The room was very dark, and we didn't have electric light. We lit ourselves with a candle or a kerosene lamp. The little house had a small kitchen in front of the corridor and a bathroom.

My father began to have problems with his legs. He used to work very hard and in a very cold environment, so he developed a very bad arthritis. He could barely walk. Knowing that there was no future for the children there, one day, the eight children and their parents took a second-class train to Tijuana. What a sad day that was for me, the oldest of the family; I was not a happy child there, but I loved school. I was a very good student, and my "padrinos" (God-parents) had promised me to pay for my education in order for me to become a teacher. My fifth-grade teacher, a wonderful teacher, told me, "Please, continue with your education." "Do not let any barriers stop you from making your dream come through." As little as I knew, I was not going to go back to school until I became an adult.

The trip was quite an experience. The nights were very cold, and we had no coats or blankets to cover ourselves. The days were hot and we would open the windows and feel the heat and the dirt in our faces. The trip was very uncomfortable. We had only two seats for the whole family. I was the oldest child, and I was only 11 years of age. Rosa is three years younger, and Angel is after her. Ricardo was five years younger than I. Conchita was born when Ricardo turned three. Irene was born after Concha, and so on.

It took us three days and nights to get to our destiny. Two wooden, uncomfortable seats on the train for the whole family, was what we were able to pay. At night, we would put the smaller children between seats to sleep. It was extremely cold, and I was not able to sleep.

There were many people selling food at the train station. We wanted to eat everything we saw, but our budget was so small that my father would buy just enough for each of us. At one of the train stops, there was a man selling "paletas"(Ice cream). We wanted one so bad that my father bought each of us one "paleta." My father had no change to pay for it. He gave the man selling them a twenty pesos bill, and the man left running to get change. Of course, he never came back. He knew that the train had to leave, and we could not wait for him to bring us the change. That was a very sad experience for us. Twenty pesos was a lot of money for us. We could have bought so much with them. That was the most sour "paleta" I ever ate!!

We finally got to Tijuana, we were to live with our maternal grandmother and her two younger children. We did not last long there. The first time that my father got drunk, He got into a fight with my grandmother, and the family was out on the street.

I did not like Tijuana. Leon was a much prettier city. We were in a Colonia upon the hills. The roads and streets were full of dirt, rocks, and holes. I desperately wanted to go back to my old house, to my school, to my life, which, after all, was not as bad as this new life.

My tio Chava (Salvador), the youngest of my mom's family, knew someone who rented a small room for five dollars per month, and he rented it for us. If it wasn't for him, I have no idea what we could have done. The room was very small, and the walls were full of holes, and we would wake up with our faces full of dirt. The room was completely empty. Our uncle brought us some pots, a little petroleum stove, and a few plates. Someone gave us some old man's coats and rags, and the family would sleep on the floor.

The worst part of the whole situation was that our mother left for California with my father's sister. It seemed that, at that point, it was the only way to bring the whole family to the United States of America. I, the oldest, became the mother of the seven children. There I was, only eleven years of age, in charge of all the children. The youngest was only six months old.

I was not told what to do or how to take care of so many little children. At first, the younger boys would get sick to the stomach very often. "The little mother," as everyone called me, began to ask questions about what to do to the neighbors. I was very lucky. The women around our family were very helpful. My father used to cook the beans and the tortillas for everyone. The (little mother) used to take care

63

of all the children. The washing of clothes had to be done by hand. In the winter, the water was so cold that my hands would freeze, and I was not able to move my fingers. The water needed to be carried up the hill in buckets. Long lines of people would wait for their turn to get water.

Tijuana was not a friendly city. The city was famous for its corrupt people. The hardest part of all this was that when the mother left, she was already pregnant with another child, and because of her situation, she was not able to come for a long time to see the children in Tijuana.

"Why did we leave Leon?" The little mother was talking to her father, "I hate Tijuana; it is so ugly, and I hate to set the bed every day. It takes me more than an hour to fix a little space for each child with all these old rags." I was so very tired. I was not going to school, the only thing that I ever enjoyed. I remember a night when we were asleep; suddenly, we felt water falling on us. The roof of the little room was taken by the wind, and it was raining very hard. It was also very dark and we had no electricity, so it was very dark. We, afraid and cold, began to cry. There was no place to go. My father noticed that there was one little corner that was dry, so we folded some of the old rugs that made our beds and placed them in that small corner. The younger children were placed there to protect them from the rain. The rest of us covered ourselves as much as we could and waited until the sun came out. That was the worst night that I have ever lived.

How sad to have to grow up so fast! It was like that even in Leon, when I had to rush home after school because my mother was waiting for me with many chores. The worst thing was that the diapers that I had to wash were pieces of old dark rags. I was called Picha then, a name that I hated). I admired the beautiful white clothing that would hang from the neighbor's clothing lines. The dishes that I had to wash were ugly, old, greasy ones. Nothing in our house was pretty. The house was an old, dark one. There were only two beds. My parents' bed had a mattress the children's did not.

I had to help my mother with the caring of children. There was always a new baby and one older child (Usually a year old) to take care of. Being the oldest of the family was no fun. My best friend's life was very different than mine. She had a much smaller family, and she was not responsible for her siblings. My friend's name was Laura. I also envy her name. I wanted to get together with her and be able to stay after school to play sports. One day I stayed after

65

school to play baseball with my friends. My mother went to get me, and she hit me in the face in front of my friends. What an embarrassment that was!! After that, my friends used to say that I had a mean mother, and I did. I was not able to get together with friends to listen to the radio and work on our beautiful needlework. I always wanted to do that, but instead, I had to go home to my cold, demanding mother and work.

Work is all I remember in Leon, but that was better than Tijuana, where I had much more responsibilities. My father continues drinking. He would go down to "El Centro" and spend the whole day and part of the night there. I can remember clearly the last time that Uncle Luis went to see us. Uncle Luis was very good to the children. When he visited us, he would bring all kinds of goodies to us. We were very happy when he and his family came to visit. We had a lot of food and goodies. Those days were very special for us.

One weekend, my tio Luis and his family came to visit, and he spent the whole day with us. At night, they left for Los Angeles. My father went with them to see them go. He did not come back during the night. For some reason, Uncle Luis's family did not leave and came back to visit the children again on Sunday morning. Uncle Luis was very surprised to find out that my father was not there and that we were by ourselves all this time. "How can someone be so irresponsible and leave these poor children by themselves?" he was crying and hitting the wall with his fist! Uncle Luis left to look for my father. He was in jail, and he was picked up by the police for fighting. He had also spent all the money given to him the day before. After that, Uncle Luis never went to visit the children again. That was a great loss for them.

CHAPTER 4

THE BIG CHANGE

We didn't spend much time in the "House with the Hole," as we called it. My mother had the idea that we should move to Tijuana, where my grandmother Josefa and my uncles Angelita and Chava were. Initially, my father flatly refused. He, who had never left Leon, not even to the Capital, to move all the way to the border, never! But seeing that he was very sick with rheumatism, almost unable to walk, he finally agreed. My father decided to ask for help from his relatives in the United States. He had me write a letter to my Aunt Celestina, his sister, telling her that he was very ill and needed financial help to move to Tijuana, with the idea of crossing into the United States since my mother was born in California. Aunt Celestina sent my father $100 dollars that she gathered from her children and some of the Sandoval, my father's cousins. This move from Leon to Tijuana was decisive in the life of all of us, as over time, we moved to the United States, the Land of Opportunities, and we did have the chance to progress each one of us. Most of my siblings through study, a lot of work, and great difficulties and sacrifices, managed to become very outstanding professionals.

It was incredible that my mom managed to convince my dad to leave Leon since he never considered her opinion in anything he did. But more than anything, it was the vision my mom had to take her family out of a place where her children would have very few opportunities to progress. All the well-being and progress that the Sistos Family has achieved, we owe to that moment when my mom had the magnificent idea of going out to look for a better life!

"What do you mean we're leaving, Mom? To where? To Tijuana, to your grandmother Pepa's house." But why, Mom? I don't want to leave Leon, here are all my friends and my school. - Yes, school was the only thing I had when my mom wouldn't let me go to school because I had to stay home and take care of my little siblings while my mom went on errands. I cried a lot because I didn't want to miss a single day of school. "But why are we leaving, Mom? Because your father is sick with rheumatism, don't you see how slowly he walks? The humidity where he works is doing him a lot of harm." — But going to my grandmother Pepa's house, my uncle Chava, and my Aunt Angelita? I remember

69

them when they lived in Union De San Antonio, Jalisco, and we used to visit them during school vacations. Do you remember, Mom? It was a long bus ride, the only one I took before we went to Tijuana. I was very happy, "What joy to not have the concern of the weekends!" Nor to have so much work after school, there it was all about playing on those beautiful full moon nights, where the nights seemed like days, playing and playing without any worries, with all the other kids. We played enchanted games, blind hen, snake of the sea and so many and so many games. "What a difference when we are in Leon. As soon as my dad gets home from work, we have to go inside and go to sleep even though the sun is still high." Those were our only vacations, the only place we went, but my dad never went with us. I didn't miss him. I felt so free; those were the days I remember without fear or anguish.

By then, Juan Ignacio, the youngest of the Eight, had been born. He was about six months old when we left Leon. At first, we called him Nachito for Ignacio, but since he was also named Juan when my father decided that we were going to Tijuana, he told us, "From now on, no more Nachito. His name is Juan, like your grandfather Juan." He did this to get along well with my mama, Pepa, and her family.

Juanito is also one of the blondes in the family. He had blue eyes, which stayed that color until he was six months old. My Aunt Ofelia said, "They won't change now. He's almost past six months," but they did change. His eyes are very clear but not blue. None of us had the eyes that my dad and my Aunt Ofelia wanted. What I never knew was if my Aunt Ofelia also checked the color of her children's eyes, none of them had colored eyes either. Now I imagine how my mom felt, having so many children, none of them were to my dad's liking.

My parents sold some furniture that was quite old, as some were inherited by my dad from his parents, and we prepared to leave Leon. I was in my fifth year at Josefa Ortiz de Dominguez School, a government school for girls only. I was very diligent in school my grades were excellent. My fourth and fifth-year teacher was named Dionicia, but we called her Miss Nicha. The teacher made sure to seat me on the first bench of the classroom, as I couldn't see from a distance. As I studied a lot, during the oral exams, the teacher sat me between two girls who knew almost nothing so that I could help them. The final exams were oral. We had to answer questions and go to the blackboard. I prepared very well and had a very good memory. The teacher

71

told us to raise our hands when they asked us questions, even if we didn't know the answers. She already knew whom to ask, and she asked me quite a bit. Important people attended the final exams, it was a special day for me, because that day I had a new dress and my mom styled my hair very nicely, but above all, I excelled in my class, as I knew almost all the answers to the questions they asked. "Felicitas, now that you're leaving, don't stop studying as you have been. If you continue as you are, you can fulfill your dream of becoming a teacher. Promise me you won't abandon school."

"I promise you, Miss Nicha, you know I like studying a lot." I didn't know that day was the last day I attended school for a very long time.

My Tia Ofelia was very sad because her dear Hermamito (Little brother) was leaving Leon. She invited us to her house and made a meal for our entire family. That was the only time my mom and Ricardo's children visited her house. My Aunt's family had many friends who had money. My Aunt's family had many large parties, where they invited a lot of people, even a bishop, as my Tio (Uncle) Checo, my Aunt's husband, had a brother who was a priest. At these parties, only my dad went. I remember very well when my cousins Lourdes and Yolanda had their first communion.

72

They had a big party with lots of food and a huge cake with two dolls, a blonde and a brunette like them. I never saw it. I only imagined it. I also didn't taste the cake or the delicious mole, not even a little bite did my Aunt Ofelia send us. We didn't even get the crumbs that were left over. My Tia Ofelia said she loved us very much, but knowing how poor we were, she never shared her good fortune with us. She never sent anything to my dad. She only invited him almost every eight days, on Sundays, to lunch. She kept food for him from the dinner they had the day before. Sometimes, my dad didn't go to my Aunt on Sundays, as he had a tremendous hangover on Saturday and woke up very ill. Then he sent my mom to my Aunt's house to bring him lunch, but it was only for him. We only watched and craved what he ate, as we were longing for everything.

Some Fridays, my dad sent me to my Tia's house to deliver some finishing records that he had saved from his tasks as a finisher and sold them to my uncle Checo. When I was on my way to my Tia's house, I was cleaning my legs and arms with saliva, as my skin was very dry from the cold and the lack of some cream that could help me. "Mi hijita (My daughter), you can wash your arms and your face." How embarrassed I was when my Tia told me that! Even so, my cousins received me well at their house and I liked going with them because life in that house was very different from mine. There, they had plenty to eat. Occasionally, they offered me a glass of milk with cookies, which tasted like glory to me. I used to save some cookies and candy to share with my mom and siblings when I got back home. Every time I could get something special to eat, I thought of my mom and brothers and sisters.

"What sadness that you are leaving, Hermanito? When will I see you again?" "Yes, Hermanita, we are leaving tomorrow. We will take the train from Guadalajara to Mexicali, and from there, we will go to Tijuana." My Tia Ofelia cried as if my dad had died. My Tia told my mom, "You are taking my 'hermanito' (little brother) way from me; you will be responsible if he gets lost in that horrible place (Tijuana). Who will be able to control him when he drinks?"

It hurt me a lot to leave Leon and, more than anything, not be able to continue my studies at my beloved school. "Felicitas, for what you love most, don't stop studying wherever you go. You have a great future, your grades are always very good, and someday you can be what you want to be, a teacher." "Miss Nicha, I promise you that I will continue studying, and yes, someday, I will be a teacher like you." I didn't know that I would not be able to return to school for many years. I didn't even finish the fifth year, I, who wanted to study a lot, didn't set foot in a school until I was in California and started studying English in night classes. By then, I was about to turn seventeen!

My Tio Checo, my Tia Ofelia's husband, accompanied us to Guadalajara to catch the train that would take us to Mexicali.

Later, mi tio told me that when he saw the train leave, he told himself, "What kind of experiences those poor children would have to suffer?" He knew my dad well and knew that my father was not capable of taking care of us children.

MAMA CHIQUITA

At last, we arrived in Tijuana. My grandmother Pepa's house was pleasant. I remember that the first day we ate there, they made a delicious broth; I had never eaten a broth with so many vegetables and so much meat, and the noodle soup was excellent. To me, it tasted like a celebration after having spent so many days eating very little. I was happy in that house, but my joy was short-lived because my father got drunk one day and fought with Old Ramon. Old Ramon was the husband of my mom's second Aunt,

Aunt Sebastiana, who owned the house that my mom's brother Jesus rented for my grandmother Pepa, my uncle Chava, and my Aunt Angelita live in, with the condition that Old Ramon also lived there. It seems that Old Ramon had gotten into trouble with U.S. law and was deported to Mexico; he could never return to the U.S. again. Old Ramon kicked us out of the house because my father, as offensive as he was when drunk, deeply insulted him. Once again, my father's drunkenness caused us pain and shame, a lot of shame. How was it possible that my father spoiled everything once more? Until when did my siblings and I have to endure the fights and the violence caused by my father's recklessness? What great pain and embarrassment! Suddenly, we found ourselves all in the street. "What are we going to do, Uncle Chava? Where are we going to go if we don't know anyone here?" "I just rented a room for you with a friend of mine." How things turn out, my uncle Chava, so young yet more mature than my father, and with his money, he rented us a room. And what a room it was! If the house in Leon where we lived was dark and ugly, it was beautiful compared to our new home. A small room, the walls made of bare wood, we could see the bare beams. The walls had holes everywhere. The first morning we woke up there, our faces were covered in dirt because the room was very close to the dirt road where trucks from downtown passed by, kicking up dust every time they drove in front of our "house." From then on, that's how we woke up every day we lived there. Every morning, I cleaned my little siblings' faces so they could open their eyes. What great sadness, we had left our land to come so far to seek a better life, but we had to live in such deplorable conditions during our first months in Tijuana. Now I wonder: Why didn't my father do anything to improve our living conditions? He didn't even think to cover the holes in the walls with cardboard or newspapers. Nothing, he did nothing. In Tijuana, jobs were scarce, but my father also did not make the effort to look for work. Some of our relatives from California brought us used clothes, and my father sold them on the streets; at first, he was embarrassed, but he, so shy, ended up selling second-hand clothes on the streets! The first few months we had no beds. In our little room, with a wooden floor, there was only the stove and the dishes that my uncle Chava bought us. Everything was in a large wooden box in a corner of the room. In another corner were boxes with the clothes my father sold and our clothes. And in another corner hung old men's sacks, which we used as blankets to keep warm. Every evening, I "made the bed"; I had to lay out all sorts of old rags on the floor to create a little space for each of my siblings and my father. An older sibling next to a younger one to keep them warm! It took me more than an hour every day, but the places were quite comfortable.

"Where is my mom going? Why is she going with my Tia Celestina?" "She's going to the Other Side, she was born in California and has papers to go there, then she will send for us, but first we need to sort out papers so we can go." So, my mom left without telling us anything, and suddenly, I had to take care of my siblings. I was eleven and a half years old, Rosa, my sister, was three years younger than me, and Juanito, the youngest of the eight siblings, was just over six months old! What a sad day that was for me. It was as if the sun had set and everything had turned gray! "What am I going to do with so many little children?" My mom didn't tell me what to do or how to prepare their food. She just left, just like that.

If we had known we wouldn't see our mom for months, we would have been even sadder. The weeks passed and turned into months and my mom didn't come. What we didn't know was that when my mom went to California, she was pregnant again! She couldn't find work because of it and didn't have money, although now that I think about it, I really don't know why she didn't come to see us, as some of my dad's relatives went to Tijuana and visited us. My mom returned to Tijuana with a new little girl named Gloria Guadalupe.

Every day, I had to carry water from a faucet at the bottom of the hill where we lived. After queuing up to fill the buckets with water, I had to carry the water and store it in tubs until there was enough for daily use. It had to be done every day, as I washed clothes daily, with two kids in diapers and all the others, and clothes got very dirty since we were surrounded by just dirt. Sometime later, Landin, the owner of the little house where we lived, built a large water tank, and then, we started buying water trips among all those who lived on Landin's property. At least then, we didn't have to carry water every day.

Landin and his wife Juanita had several children: Lupe, the eldest, the second child, was called Vicente, but they called him Titon. La Chuchena, a chubby, very mischievous and quarrelsome girl, and two other small children. Juanita was a very thin and very young woman. It seems that she married Landin when she was almost a child, and he was much older than her. When I met them, he was already an old man, but he was a strong and hard-working man and always kept himself busy. He was the owner of the little house where we lived and also had some new but poorly made apartments, as they were two-story and had no way to get up to the second floor. He rented the apartments below, but those above were always empty because to go up, people needed to climb a shaky and old ladder, with the risk of falling, so nobody wanted to live upstairs. Juanita was a very good mother and a very hardworking wife. She had her house very clean. I began to notice how Juanita did her work and learned a lot from her. I observed how she took care of her children, how she cleaned her house, and learned to wash clothes as she did. From the beginning, when we arrived at the little house, Landin's children made our lives difficult. "They were terrible!

"Picha, Picha," - That's what they called me, a nickname I never liked because the kids in Leon made fun of me, saying: "Neither pitch nor catch nor let bat." Even the children of my Aunt Chavela made fun of my nickname. But it was all my Aunt Ofelia's idea. When she knew they named me Felicitas like her mother, she told my dad, "We have to call her Picha because that's what they called my mom," and her wishes were commands. Of course, she didn't name her children Concha, Victorio, Angel, or Felicitas, as my dad did, to honor the names of his parents and siblings. She named her daughters Lourdes, Yolanda, Magdalena, etc. "Those kids are bothering us a lot. They say many bad words, throw stones at us, and don't leave us in peace. "Don't pay attention to them; those kids are bad, and the Devil will take them away for being bad. Did you see what they did the other day? - They entered the house and urinated and dirtied our blankets, but God will punish them! "If they say nasty things, tell them that snakes are coming out of their mouths." So little by little, telling them stories of very bad people who were damned and describing Hell to them, the children of Landin and Juanita began to change. Lupe, the oldest, changed so much that she no longer wanted to go outside to play and spent the day praying for the Souls in Purgatory to escape their suffering and for God to take them to Heaven. That's how our life in Tijuana went.

My Aunt Angelita, my mom's younger sister, had a daughter whom she named Maria Elena. She never wanted to say who the father was, no matter how much they tried to get the truth from her. She and her daughter stayed to live with my uncle Chava and my grandmother Pepa. Years later, my Aunt Angelita left with Rogelio, the brother of Raymundo, the owner of the house where they had moved months before. My uncle Rogelio told us years later that Maria Elena was the daughter of Old Ramon. Finally, it was proven what my uncle Chava had asserted for so long. "Dad, I'm going to iron clothes at my grandmother Pepa's house," "Yes, but don't be late. Juanito misses you so much when you're not here." Every Friday, I went with a pile of clothes.

A little girl was born in California. She was named Gloria. My mother had had a very bad time while waiting for this child. She had lived with several of the relatives. She ended up living with one of her sister's neighbors, who was kind enough to offer her a roof. This good lady took care of her during the last days of her pregnancy and took her to the hospital when the time came.

Gloria was a beautiful, big brown eyes girl. She was named after the Samaritan who had been so good to my mother. This person became Gloria's Godmother and fell in love with her.

The Godmother wanted to adopt Gloria: "Comadre, you have many children in Tijuana; you cannot take care of them because you have to be here and work. I will take care of Gloria, but you will need to give her to me." That was true, but they were not able to give Gloria away, and she was taken to Tijuana with the rest of the children.

Gloria was fine for a while, but she was used to another way of life and became sick. She lost a lot of weight, did not want to eat, and was always sick of her stomach. She was not taken to the doctor soon enough, and she died. When my father found out how sick Gloria was, he called my mother and told her to come to Tijuana to take Gloria back to Los Angeles, where she was born, so she could be taken to the doctor. My mother came for Gloria and took her with her. She took a bus to Los Angeles. They were halfway there way when my mother noticed that Gloria was not moving. Mom did not know what to do. Gloria was dead! My mother got off the bus at the next stop and came back to Tijuana. It was a horrible day for all of us. We couldn't believe that our beautiful little sister was dead. What a terrible feeling of guilt for "little mother." For many years, I felt like it was my fault that Gloria died because I was not able to take good care of her, but I was still a child myself.

To make things worse, my father did not come back home, and there we were with a dead little girl, not knowing what to do. When my father finally came home, my mother and he left, taking Gloria with them. We never knew what happened to her. They probably buried her.

CHAPTER 5

COMPLETELY ALONE

When my dad went to California to work alongside my mom, we moved in with my mama Pepa and my tios. By then, I was about fourteen years old. "Picha, today I can't help you with the chores. My head hurts too much," she said. What a coincidence! When it wasn't her head, it was her stomach, or, according to my Tia Angelita, she had a fever—she never helped me wash, clean the house, or cook. I had to do everything, not just our laundry but also wash the clothes of my grandma Pepa my tio Chava, and even she wanted me to wash her and her daughter's clothes. I also had to cook and clean the house. My mom was paying her to help me, but she gladly took the money my mom sent for her and stayed very calm. Sure enough, in the afternoon, once I had somewhat finished the work, she would get up and get ready because she was trying to make a good impression on Don Raymundo's bachelor brother. "I feel better now. I'm going out to talk with Rogelio. If Rogelio's mom or sister come by, let me know because they don't like me and

85

don't like me talking to Rogelio." Of course, they didn't like her; everyone knew how lazy she was and how I had to do everything. Besides, she had a baby and no one knew who the father was. "It's not fair, Picha. Why doesn't Aunt Angelita help you with the work if my mom is paying her to help you?" I don't know, Angel, but now I'm worse off than when we were alone." "Tia, why don't you help Picha with the work if my mom pays you to look after us and help, and you spend all day lying down or getting ready?" "What do you care, you rude boy? You have no right to tell your Tia anything. Shut up and go outside." Both my Grandma Pepa and my Tia Angelita would scold Angel, my brother, for defending me, but he kept telling them: "When my mom comes, I will tell her what's happening, Grandma Pepa, you know I'm right, that you are taking advantage of my sister." "Tell whatever you want to your mom, you nosy boy, get out. I don't want to see you here." Angel was always very brave and defended his siblings whenever it was necessary. "What's going on? Why are you arguing with this boy? You are a grown woman, and you're picking on a kid?" "Chava, this boy is rude and meddles in what doesn't concern him." "It does concern him because he's right, Angelita, you are lazy, and Irene is paying you to help Picha with the work, and instead, she now has more work than before." "Well, if they don't like it, they can go back to their house." "But mom, don't be unfair. These kids also take care of you. When you go to the store, Rosita always goes with you because you shouldn't go alone in case you have an attack, and who would help you?" Also, when you have your attacks, they are ready to help you get up. It was true. We lived on the edge, always on alert that Grandma Pepa wouldn't fall over because we never knew when she was going to have an epileptic seizure, and it was very traumatic for us to see her convulsing on the ground, foaming at the mouth; we were afraid she would choke. It was very difficult for us!

After a while, my mom came to visit us, and we told her about the situation with my Aunt Angelita. My mom agreed that it was better for us to live alone. We went back to renting from Landin, and now we could afford two rooms in the apartments he had. We bought two beds, a stove, and kitchen utensils. Now, I took care of the shopping and the money our parents sent us went a long way. We ate like we had never eaten before; milk, eggs, bread, and I made good stews because I could ask Juanita how to make this dish or that! Everything was much better for us. My older siblings went to school, and they got very good grades as they were very studious. I stayed with Vito and Juan because they were not old enough for school. I took care of the household chores, laundry, looking after the children, and cooking. For me, and as some of my siblings remember, those were the best days we lived in Tijuana because we didn't have to worry about my dad, no one scolded us, and we took care of everything we had to do. In the evenings, after we finished eating and everyone had done their homework, some neighbors would come over, and we would put music on a small record player that we had, and we would dance.

GLORIA GUADALUPE

I don't quite remember what happened next, but I was given the opportunity to return to California, and I arrived at my Aunt Josefina's place, my mom's sister. From there, I went to work with Gloria, looking after her children. Gloria was a neighbor of my Aunt Felicitas, my mom's sister, and was the comadre of my parents (in Mexico, the Godparents are called compadres of the children's parents) as she and her husband Joe were the godparents of Gloria Guadalupe, the first girl born in California when we had just recently arrived in Tijuana. It was during the time we did not see my mom for many months until one day, they brought me Lupita to take care of. Lupita was about 3 months old. According to my mom, Gloria, her godmother, wanted them to give Lupita to her, as she had helped my mom during her pregnancy and took care of Gloria from newborn so that my mom could work and send us money to Tijuana, as we depended on what she sent. Gloria grew fond of Lupita and wanted to adopt her. My parents decided to bring her to Tijuana instead of giving her to Gloria. Lupita could not withstand the harsh life in Tijuana; she was used to the care she received in her first months of life. In Tijuana, the little house where we lived was very cold; the dirt came in from all sides, and I didn't know how to take care of her. When they left me with Juanito, six months old, and Vito, two years old, I did the best I could with them. Juanito was almost always sick with stomach issues, but he survived despite the poor care. Lupita didn't, as she was more fragile and could not survive the hardship the rest of the children were able to endure.

I returned once more to California to work taking care of the children of Gloria and Joe, my parents' compadres. I was only there for a short time, as a friend to whom I gave the address where I was staying called immigration on me, as I had passed with a local passport and should not have been working with it. Comadre Gloria convinced the immigrants to let me go and that they would return me to my home. By that time, we were already in the process of arranging our legal documents to enter the United States. The day we had the appointment to arrange the documents, we were surprised to find out that we qualified for American citizenship because my mom was an American citizen, and we entered the United States as Naturalized Americans. That was very good for us as we did not have to pay for immigrant visas. We arrived in Pacoima, California, in June 1962. By that time, we were no longer just eight siblings; we were nine, as Gerardo had been born in February of that same year in California. We all arrived in different groups; some came with my mom and arrived with my Tia Celestina in Burbank, where my dad was, and another group arrived with Lolilla and her husband David in Pacoima. We were separated for several days. It was very hard getting used to a way of life so different from what we were used to. For the people we arrived with, it was also difficult as they saw us as savages who did not know how to behave.

Before all this happened, my parents decided that in order to be able to take all the children across the border, both parents needed to be working in the United States. My father left to meet with my mother and both started to work in a rich house in Beverly Hills. The children were sent to live with their maternal grandmother and her younger children. The children's younger Aunt had become an unwed mother and had a little girl. The youngest of their uncles was also living there. The children were sent there to be protected so the "little mother" could get some help from her Aunt with the heavy load of work that seven children generated. It did not work. The Aunt was very lazy, and the "little mother" not only needed to do her work but ended up cooking and washing clothes for the grandmother and her children. Although the Aunt was being paid to help with the work, she did not do much. Also, Angel, the oldest of the boys, used to get very upset with the way things were and confronted the grandmother and the Aunt.

Angel was the Angel of the family. He honored his name. He had a very big heart. When the family was in Leon, he was just a little boy. The mother had noticed that he was coming a little late from school and went to pick him up and to find out what he was doing after school. She was surprised to see him going into a church by himself and praying. After, he would go to the collection box and put the few cents that he was given to spend. Angel is not afraid of his Aunt and grandmother, but they mistreat him and make his life miserable. This took place for a while, until one day, the young uncle was able to listen to the way both women treated Angel. The uncle defended him, and things changed for Angel. The rest of the situation continued the be the same.

The next time that our mother came to see us, she was told about the situation of the family with the grandmother and the Aunt. My mother decided that it would be better for the children to be by themselves. We went back to our previous home, which was made bigger. One more room was added to it, and it was fixed. It did not have any more holes in the wall. We finally had beds and other furniture. That was the best time that we had in Tijuana. Our father was not there anymore, and we did not have to worry about him getting drunk. We were able to eat better and had better clothes. We were finally free of embarrassment for our father's behavior.

Neighbors were amazed to see such mature children being able to take care of each other at such a young age.

Many times, the older kids fought other kids to defend the younger ones. Especially Rosa, she was very tough and defended her siblings whenever was needed. I had grown up and had more experience. I was a Teenager and had matured a lot. I used to do my work during the day, and when all the kids came back from school, ate dinner, and did their chores, we would get together with friends and dance.

Vito, the second youngest, was a very good dancer. Everyone respected him even though he was just a little boy. We thought that he was special because of what happened the morning that he was born. It was very early in the morning. It was still very dark when he was born back in Leon. The children were sent to the kitchen. It was very small, and the older children's heads were outside the kitchen's doors. We were looking at the stars when we saw a falling star, and at that moment, we heard a baby's cry. The brothers and sisters thought that he was a very special little boy because the star fell the moment Vito was born. He also had a twisted tuft of hair in his fourth head, and whenever there was a situation that needed clarification, Vito would say, "he or she did it," and no one would doubt him.

93

The children who were going to school in Tijuana enjoyed school and were getting very good grades. One time, when Ricardo went to the doctor to have his tonsils taken off, the doctor asked him about his grades. He was having all A's, and the doctor did not believe it. The next time Ricardo went to see him took his grades to show him. The doctor told him, "You are very smart and can get to be whatever you want to be in life." Ricardo answered, "Yes, I know, I am going to be a doctor" This Idea had come to him for the first time when his sister Gloria died.

We had no idea how to go about getting legal documents to enter The United States.

It took us more than five years to be able to come to this country. We were told that we needed to apply for immigration documents. In order to do that, a lot of money was needed to pay for the visas for each child. Another child was born during this time. He was named Gerardo after an ex-boyfriend of the "comadre" Gloria. Gerardo was the first of the four children that were born in California. He was an American Citizen!

When we went to the interview at the immigration department, the person who conducted the interview told my parents that all eight children qualified for American Citizenship due to the fact that my mother was born in the United States of America. Our Mexican Birth Certificates were stamped, and my parents were told, "Welcome to the United States of America." my father asked, "Can we all go to California now?' The officer told him, "Yes, you can."

We could not believe that the process was so easy. We started walking to the borderline between Tijuana, Mexico, and San Isidro, USA. We went to "El otro Lado" (the other side) with no problem, just showing our stamped birth certificate.

The first part of our dream was accomplished. My parents were also very happy because they saved the payment of the immigration process and the expensive visas.

I was amazed at how clean, green, and beautiful the other side was. It seemed that I was dreaming. Those houses were beautiful with their green gardens and flowers all over the place!

In July of 1962, the children came in two different groups. The first group was taken to the house of the father's sister. The second group was taken to the house of cousins David and Lola. In the first group came Rosa, the second sister, Ricardo, Angel, the oldest boy, and Concha. They were placed in the garage because they were full of lice. The children were very embarrassed when my tia cleaned their heads with a very strong insecticide. They were not able to get inside the house until they were completely cleaned.

My tia's younger boy had Down Syndrome. The children had never seen anybody like him and were afraid of him. When one of the boys was asked if he wanted to go with the rest of the children, he gladly went. The relatives who took him had a boy who bothered him a lot, but he would rather deal with him than stay where he was.

The youngest of the eight coming from Tijuana was six years old and the older kids were from one to two years apart. They all were at cousins David and Lola's house.

David helped the family settle in a house next to them. It was a one-bedroom house. It was too small for them, but it was the only thing available to them. The family was very active at their church, and their children attended the catholic school. They used their influence there, and five of the children started elementary school in a private school. The older children were placed with younger children. They felt embarrassed because not only were they too big for the grades they were in, but they did not understand anything that was happening in the classroom. They were placed at the doors so children would not leave the classrooms. David also helped them develop credit to buy furniture.

Once, we were in California; one day, I told my brothers and sisters, "I do not like to be called Picha. My name is Felicitas, and I would like to be called Feli. Every time you call me Feli, I will give you twenty cents."

Everyone went to school except the "little mother," who was not the mother anymore. After being in charge of all the children for more than five years, the real mother told the children, "I am your mother, Feli is not. You come to me for everything," but the children were so used to going to now, sister, for everything that they continue to go to her for everything they needed or wanted. Mother and daughter became rivals. The mother resented the oldest daughter a lot, and the daughter did not like her mother at all.

At first, even though the little mother was told that she was not the children's mother, the parents left her with the younger children, who were not going to school. The youngest was Lalo who was born a few months before. No one thought that she was only sixteen years of age and had the right to attend school. Some of the family's relatives spoke to the parents about the situation, and the parents decided to send Feli to work and for the mother to stay home with her children.

CALIFORNIA

Later, my mom returned; I think she was pregnant and came to stay with us, but I was sent to my Aunt Celestina's place so that I could work looking after children and make some money in Los Angeles, California. I spent some time working with the children of Ramiro, my cousin, the son of my Aunt Celestina. They treated me well there. Every weekend, I went to my Aunt Celestina's house, where Lupe, Vicky, and Aggie, my cousins, children of my Aunt Cele, and my uncle Jose, were also staying. My Aunt Celestina was very gossipy and wasn't very kind to me, but my Uncle Jose, on the other hand, was a fair person, and I felt more confident with him than with my Aunt. Agustin, who was called Aggie, had a mental delay but was very bold, and I didn't trust him much, yet he was very spoiled. After some time, they called me back to Tijuana, as my mom had a miscarriage, and they needed me once again to take care of my siblings.

CHAPTER 6

OUR FIRST HOUSE

Finally, we rented a small one-bedroom house next to Lola and David in Pacoima; it was our intention to buy it, but it didn't occur to us that it was too small for 11 people. We were used to living all cramped together. Fortunately, for some reason, we couldn't buy it, and the deal didn't go through, thank God! After some time, we found a brand-new house with three bedrooms and two bathrooms, a mansion for us! And the best part was that we were able to buy it. We had the money my parents had saved for the eight visas, which weren't needed. By then, I was already working in a sewing factory. I was only seventeen years old, but when we filled out the application, we put that I was 18 years old, and I got the job. At first, I didn't like my new life; it was so different from what I had experienced in Tijuana. For more than five years, I was the mother to my siblings. I took care of everything. I fixed their clothes and sent them to school, and when my dad also came to California, I also took care of the shopping, cooking, and making sure all my siblings did their homework—in a word, everything. When my mom first came to the United States, Juanito, the youngest of the 8 of us who came from Leon, was 6 months old. Vito, the second youngest, was two years old, and so on, up to me, who was 12 years old. When we all arrived in California, my mom told my siblings, "I am your mom. Picha (that's me) is not; don't ask her what to do. You have to ask me because I am your mom." I felt like my heart was torn apart, and I thought, "How can she leave her children for so many years for me to take care of them, and suddenly I am nobody to my siblings?" I didn't understand how such a thing could be happening if my mom, when she would visit us in Tijuana, wouldn't even ask how we were, didn't tell us she missed us, nor did she help me with so much work that I had, she was like a visitor who came occasionally. She and my dad would go out, and we continued with our lives as always. A few times, they took us to the park, but my mom remained distant, like a stranger to me, just like in Leon, and now, after so long, she wanted to have all the rights with "her children." For a long time, I had a lot of resentment towards my mom, and to some extent, we became rivals, as my siblings didn't trust her and kept coming to me to tell me their things, and she didn't like that. My mom worked for a while, and we left Juanito and Gerardo with a lady named Dona Nacha to take care of them, but she didn't take good care of them. The children looked very sad and neglected. Later, we found out that this woman abused Lalo, which caused him a trauma that lasted a long time. After Tere was born, my mom stayed home to take care of the younger ones. I think that transition was difficult for my mom. For more than five years, she didn't have to take care of little kids, just work to send us money to Tijuana, and suddenly she had the obligation again. She didn't seem happy. When she would visit us in Tijuana, she was very well-dressed and looked like a young girl. She was a young girl, as she was very young and had time to fix herself up and buy her beautiful dresses. She looked much younger than when we were in Leon. When she stayed again with the children, she stopped dressing up, gained weight, and had more children. I think she became depressed. When we came back from work, we would find the house a mess. She wouldn't even take out the kitchen trash. The food wasn't good. She didn't strive to cook anything tasty. She and I had many arguments, as I would come home tired and did-n't like to see the house dirty and I would start cleaning, but very angrily. It reached the point that once she told me,

"This is my house, and I keep it how I want. When you get married you keep your house as you want. Leave mine in peace."

A NEW ROLE

Over time, I took on my father's role because he didn't drive and didn't have a job, and I got him the job where he had worked for many years. I had to learn to drive immediately. We bought a station wagon, and I drove it, taking my father to and from work. David, my Cousin Lola's husband, took me to a furniture store and helped me establish my own credit. There, I bought all the furniture for our new house and paid it off little by little. My mom got pregnant again and was afraid to tell my dad because he no longer wanted more children, but he did nothing to prevent it since it was a sin! At that time, my dad wanted to go to Leon to see his sister and also to get surgery for an ulcer he claimed was very bad. He wanted to bring quite a bit of money to Leon. With much effort, we managed to give him a thousand dollars, which at that time was a lot of money for us. With many sacrifices, we got the money, and my dad went to Leon without knowing that my mom was expecting another child. I don't remember how long my dad spent visiting his sister. I just remember that we had a very hard time during that period. When he returned, we had to tell him about my mom's pregnancy because she was almost four months pregnant and could no longer hide it. That day, I had a big argument with my dad because he was furious with my mom, and I told him, "It's also your responsibility, not just my mom's." This made my dad almost hit me because he was not used to anyone contradicting him. The saddest part of all is that he came back from Leon without money and without having had the surgery because "The ulcer improved a lot and there was no need for the operation," and of course, he gave money to his sister and her children. By then, I had already taken my mom to the doctor, and her pregnancy was quite advanced. At that time, I would have been about 17 years old. A girl was born whom we named Teresa by majority vote; she was the third born in the United States after Gerardo. A year later, another girl was born; we named her Laura, a name I had much to do with, as Laura was the name of my best friend from Leon. In Tijuana, I no longer had friends my age, as I didn't have time to play like other girls; I was very busy taking care of my seven little siblings. The last of our family to be born was Mario, and finally, without my dad knowing, my mom asked the doctor to fix her so she wouldn't have any more children. My dad never found out what my mom did because I was the one who took her to her doctor and to the hospital when she had her children. My mom's last pregnancy was very difficult as she developed a blood clot that moved in her system and was very dangerous if it reached her brain. The doctor wanted to hospitalize her, but we didn't have the money, so she was put on complete rest at home. Those were very difficult days. Rosa and I took turns cooking and doing housework after coming home from work until our dear Mario was born.

PACOIMA

We were fortunate to move to Pacoima, the city where my dad's niece Dolores, whom we called Lolilla, lived. She was married to David, the people who helped us the most when we arrived in the United States. First, they recommended our family to the priest of the Guardian Angel church, and since David helped a lot at the church, the priest pulled some strings, and Rosa, Angel, Ricardo, Concha, and Irene, whom we call Nena, were accepted into the Catholic school. My siblings didn't have to go to public elementary school. We began living in a rented one-bedroom house, which we planned to buy because we knew it was very difficult to find a rental with so many children. My parents had saved enough money to pay for the visas when arranging documents, but it wasn't necessary to pay because the eight siblings qualified for American citizenship since my mom was born in the United States. With that money, we gave the down payment for a new three-bedroom, two-bathroom house we bought on Hoyt Street in Pacoima, where the last three children of my parents were born.

My first job was in a sewing factory, where I started ironing shirts during the hottest time. I didn't iron for long because I started attending night school to learn English, and I learned quite fast. When the foreman saw that I understood some English, he gave me the opportunity to distribute work to the seamstresses. I had to mix all the shirt parts by colors and numbers and distribute them. This job was paid by the hour. The seamstresses were paid for what they did, and some earned very good money. During my lunch hour, I began practicing on the double-needle machines, one of the most complicated machines. I wanted to earn more money because we really needed it since my dad lost his job and couldn't find one. It was very sad to come home and know that no, "my dad can't find work." Then, it occurred to me to ask my supervisor for a job for my dad. My dad started working in the warehouse of the sewing factory, earning little, but with mine, we barely made it by. When the supervisor saw me practicing the two-needle machine every day, she gave me the opportunity to work on the machine, closing shirts. At first, I was in the line of the slowest operators. At the beginning of the lines, the shirt assembly started, and at the end, the shirt came out complete. If one was very slow to sew, the people in front of them ran out of work. Little by little, I gained speed on the machine, and a few weeks later, I was operating my machine on the fastest line. I started earning quite a bit more money, but the work was very hard. I was very bad at eating, and I began to lose a lot of weight and suffer from very strong headaches. One day, we ran into a cousin on my dad's side named Evelia, called Bella, who told me I didn't look very well and asked if I was sick. I told her, "It's because I'm a sewing machine operator, and I work a lot." She, knowing my story, said, "You're already overworked and too young to work so hard. I work in electronics; the work isn't as heavy as sewing, and it pays well. Call my Aunt Catalina, my Uncle Manuel's wife; the foremen appreciate her a lot. She can get you a job." I called her, and she gladly recommended me to the supervisor, and the following Monday, I showed up at Morse Electronics for an interview. I got the job and was supposed to start work the next day. I asked for permission to arrive a bit late because I wanted to notify and thank the supervisors at the sewing factory. The next day, I went to give thanks. The supervisor said, "What do you mean you're leaving? You can't do that; I have many plans for you. You have a great future here. I want you to learn to operate all the machines and the rest of the production process. You could become a supervisor; you'd help me a lot since the current supervisors don't speak Spanish, and you're learning English very quickly, which is what I need. Besides, I gave your dad a job, and if you leave, he has to leave, too." We really needed my dad to continue working. I said, "I accept to stay; I'll come tomorrow, just going to thank them for the opportunity they're giving me." I returned to electronics, explained my situation to the new supervisor, and he asked me, "What kind of work does your dad do at the factory?" "He works in the warehouse." "You know what? Stay to work today, and bring your dad with you tomorrow." "For an interview?" "No, to work." I couldn't believe what was happening; just like that, my dad already had a better job with a much better future. That day was a very happy day for me and for the whole family. From that day, I worked at Morse until I left the job to get married. My dad worked there the rest of his days until he retired. I was very happy working at Morse; they gave me the opportunity to perform in different positions. Before I arrived, my Aunt Catalina did the most complicated jobs, but little by little, I began to do the same as her. It was never my intention to take her place; that's just how things happened. She moved to another electronics company after some time. She never said anything, but I felt bad as if I had betrayed her after she was the reason not only my dad and I were working there, but some of my siblings also worked there during vacations, as some attended high school and worked during the summer.

MY MARRIAGE

I was in a relationship with a young man named Reynaldo, who I loved very much. Our relationship lasted almost five years. Everybody assumed that we one day will be married. He was supporting his large family living in Mexico. His father was ill and could not work. I was helping my father to support our family. Due to this fact, we could not think about marriage.

My father was very strict and did not let me go out with my boyfriend by ourselves. One of my sisters would go with us. For a while, Reynaldo was okay with the situation. My sisters grew up and had their own activities and did not want to accompany us anymore. "Papa, could I go with Reynaldo to the show by ourselves?" "No, one of your sisters has to go with you." "But Papa, you know Reynaldo well; he is a good person, and he is very respectful with me, "and my sisters don't want to go with us anymore. Please let us go." I said, "No, and it is not going to change!" "Take one of your younger brothers with you." When my father said no, it was no, and he used to say NO most of the time when I asked his permission to go somewhere. I used to think, *how could I have stayed with my brothers and sisters in Tijuana for long periods of time by myself with no supervision? I was a teenager then and was capable of taking care of myself and my younger siblings, and my father was okay with that? Now I am in my twenties, I make more money than my dad, and I can't even go by myself with Reynaldo anywhere.* I wanted to tell my dad that, but I was too afraid to do it, so I followed his commands.

Reynaldo got tired of the situation, and we began to fight a lot. The situation got worse when my sister Rosa, who had been in a relationship with a boy who came from the military, told my dad that the parents of her boyfriend were going to come to ask his permission for marriage. "Picha," even though my family and friends were calling me Feli now, for him I was Picha (Like his mother's nickname). "I want to talk to you. What is it with your boyfriend? Your relationship with him has been too long. I don't think he is serious with you. When is he going to ask you to marry him?" It was true that Rosa had been in this relationship for less than a year, and she was already making plans for her wedding.

I confronted Reynaldo, and he told me, "I can't marry you now. I am the supporter of my family; I can't abandon them, just like that." I do not know when I will be able to do it, so I love you very much, but I am giving you your freedom to find someone else who can make you happy." I was very hurt and did not show my grief to him. I just agreed to end the relationship.

I suffered very much, and for almost two years, I was depressed, did not go anywhere, and did not want to have any relationship. I continued working very hard to help my family, but I did not buy beautiful clothes. Actually, I didn't take care of myself.

The day I met Francisco, who we call Pancho, I was very attracted to him. I began to trust the man again and accepted him. When he asked me to marry him after six months of our relationship, I said "YES." I did not want to have another long relationship and did not want to be an old maid, and I wanted to have my own children and family.

We married on August 23rd, 1969. Ours was a simple wedding. Only the family, but we both had big families. He had nine brothers and sisters, and I had eleven brothers and sisters. It was a memorable event.

We did not plan our future. I had a solid job, and Pancho did not. I accepted to go to live close to his family and left everything behind, I only took the few clothes that I had. I had bought a car and most of the furniture for my parent's home and I left everything to them. I also gave my parents the money that I had saved. I felt bad leaving my family without my support, but I wanted to start my own family.

I never asked Pancho how much he made or how much money he had. I soon found out that he had spent all the money he had on our wedding. He rented a one-bedroom apartment. We managed to stay for two months in it. We had to rent an apartment that had no bedroom. It was a small living room, the bed was on a closet in the wall, and the kitchen was very small.

Our son Frank was born ten months later, and a year and a half later, our second son Fernando was born when Frank turned three years old our last son Alex was born. The birth of my sons was the best gift I have ever received. My dream of having my own children had been fulfilled. After my son Alex was born, we decided to have no more children. We both came from big families and knew how hard it was and wanted our children to have a better life than ours.

Our marriage went through many difficult times. Many times, we almost ended our marriage, but we did not give up and continued working to keep it. I am very proud to say that we have been married fifty-five years!!

When we got to Pacoima, our family was living next door to my father's nice, Lola and David. Lola and David had four children about the age of the younger siblings of the family.

One day, one of the children came from school very surprised and told her mother," Mom, you should have heard Nena speaking to another child. She sounded like she had known English all her life." She was talking about the sixth girl in the line. The younger children picked up the English language very fast. According to the father, Nena was not very smart. When the time came for her to attend college. She knew that her father would never agree for her to leave home to go to school. So, Vito, one of the younger brothers, helped Nena with all the paperwork needed to apply to universities. He even fortified the father's signature when needed. Nena was accepted to St. Mary's College. She was excited but also very nervous about telling her father that she was leaving home to live on the college campus. She was not the first of the family to attend college. Angel and Ricardo were already going. For them, there was no hassle; the father believed in education for boys, but girls did not need education to get married and have children. The news was like a bomb explosion to the father. No one had ever confronted him; Nena did. She was admirable. The older girls could not believe what she was doing. What gave her the strength to pursue her dream? Maybe the terrible situation at home had something to do with it. My father told

Nena that if she left, never to come back. She had no father or family. She left the house crying. No one defended her. Everyone was afraid of my father. How terrible it must have been for her. She had never been away from home. She was alone in a new environment, thinking that she might never see her family again. She was able to overcome all the obstacles and became a teacher, a wonderful teacher who has touched many children's lives. My father "forgave her" and had to admit that she was not stupid. On the contrary, she was a very intelligent girl. After her example, all the younger girls were encouraged to study, too.

Conchita was born three years after Ricardo. She was a beautiful-eyed, curly-haired girl. When she was about six months old, her father, Ricardo, had a terrible fight with his "compadre" Domingo. What an experience that was for all those little children who had been exposed to so much violence every time their father drank. After that day, Ricardo, who was almost a baby and watched the whole fight, became very ill. He was ill for months. He became very skinny, and his skin turned yellow.

Rica became very ill and needed a blood transfusion. His father donated his blood, and after that, he was a healthy, strong little boy.

Concha, whose actual name is Concepcion, was named after one of the father's sisters. Ricardo, who was very proud of his "very handsome family', named most of his children after his family members' names. The first girl was named Felicitas, after her grandmother. Angel was named after his grandfather and his uncle, whose name was also Angel. Victorio, who we call Vito, was named after Victorio, his Great grandfather.

CHAPTER 7
OVERCOMING

My siblings were always very studious and responsible. The first to attend university was Angel. After finishing elementary school at El Angel Guardian, he began attending San Fernando High School. My parents wanted him to go to a Catholic high school, where David and Lola's children went. San Fernando High had a bad reputation because, at that time, there was a lot of friction with students from different ethnicities. But Angel said, "That school is very expensive, and we don't have the money; I'll go to the public school because when someone wants to study, they can do it anywhere." So it was. He studied a lot, using a dictionary to do his work since he still had problems with English. When he was about to graduate, he spoke with his counselor because he wanted to continue studying and needed support. The counselor told him, "The best thing you can do is take some mechanic, plumber, or other trade classes. If you go to university, you're going to fail because you're not ready to pursue a career." Angel replied, "No, I want to study Engineering. Please tell me what classes I should take and how I can prepare to have the opportunity to be accepted into a university. 'Well, if you insist, I will help you, but I think you're headed for failure." Angel began to prepare, studying more than ever. It wasn't easy, as he also worked every day after school at a dairy, even on weekends; he and Ricardo had to work until closing, which was at nine at night. It was very hard for them to work there since the city of Pacoima was not safe; there was a lot of violence and theft. They were robbed several times, being so young; the boss gave them a gun to defend themselves. Ricardo told me that when he was on his way to work, he felt like he was facing death! But there was no choice; they had to work to get ahead. The family continued to grow, and so did the expenses, and there was the only place near our house where they could work after school. The two of them had to study a lot, as they had the obstacle of the English language, which they gradually mastered. When they did their homework, they had a dictionary by their side. They also had to go to the library to study because there was no space at home, no special or private places to concentrate. I don't know how they achieved so much in so little time! Not only were they accepted into very good universities, but they also received some scholarships, and with the help of student loans, they completed their university education.

Angel was accepted at Northridge University. Around that time, he met Vicky and fell deeply in love. She also graduated from high school, and Angel advised her to prepare. She was also accepted into the university, and the two of them went to live at the university. Soon after, she became pregnant. Angel, being the responsible young man that he was and because he loved her very much, married her. "You're not going to graduate, Angel. You won't be able to continue studying with the great responsibility of a family," my father told him. "I swear to you, Dad, that I will graduate. I give you my word. No matter what happens, I will bring you my engineering graduation diploma." He and Vicky, his wife, suffered many deprivations and great sacrifices to achieve their goals. Vicky did not continue her studies because soon after, they had their first daughter, Angelica, and then Rebecca was born. Later, they had Diana, and the last was Miguel. And so, with all this happening, Angel fulfilled what he promised like a true gentleman and graduated as a mechanical engineer. Not only that, he went back to look for that counselor who tried to convince him not to pursue a career because he would fail. "You are here to support and encourage students to work towards their goals, not to dissuade them and intimidate them by giving advice that doesn't help," and he showed him his engineering diploma!

As I said before, Angel was the first in our family to have the vision and drive to attend a university. He set an example to follow, as all my siblings and I followed in his footsteps, learning that in the United States, the land of opportunities, anyone who wants to overcome, with vision, much effort, and work, can achieve what they set out to do. Ricardo was the second to follow in Angel's footsteps. He graduated from a private high school with honors and scholarships and was accepted into several of the best universities, including Harbor and Stanford. He had the luxury of choosing Stanford. The admissions department at Harbor contacted him to ask why he had decided not to go to their university, as he had spent the previous summer at Harbor, but he didn't like the humid climate, and since he had options, he chose Stanford. Not just anyone can say they didn't attend Harbor University because they didn't want to. At Stanford, Ricardo met Roberta, and they became boyfriend and girlfriend. They also married before Ricardo finished his medical career, and Robbie also left her studies because they also had their children at the same time Ricardo was finishing his career and doing his services at the hospital. Ricardo and Robbie's first child was Antonio, and Daniel was born a year later. By the time Armando was born, Ricardo had completed his service, and they moved to Washington, where Ricardo began to practice his profession. Finally, Ricardo fulfilled his dream of being a doctor. Ever since we were in Tijuana, he was about eight years old. He had a problem with his tonsils, and a doctor operated on him. That doctor asked him, "How are you doing in school? Very well, "I only get tens on my report card." "I don't believe it. Next time you come, bring it to me. Let's see if it's true." Rica brought it to him so he could see it, the doctor told him, "if you continue with such good grades, and you want to, you can be a doctor." From then on, whenever someone asked him, "What are you going to be when you grow up?". He answered, "A doctor," and Concha, who was three years younger than him, said to him, "And I'm going to be your nurse? Yes, you'll be my nurse," and so it was. He became a doctor, and graduated from one of the best universities in the United States, and Conchita was not only a nurse, but she had very important assignments, as she worked many years at the General Hospital in Los Angeles, California. For her, it was very difficult to study her career. When she was about to graduate from high school, with very good grades as well, because she is a very intelligent girl, Rosa, the next one after me, decided to get married, and my father told Conchita, "You can't continue studying because now you need to work to help the family like your sisters. For some reason, it was important to my father that the boys studied but not the girls. "You girls are going to get married, and your husbands will support you. Your brothers must study because they are going to be heads of families and must prepare." We, the eldest of the family, accepted it. I only went to night school to learn English because I had to start working before I turned 18. Rosa was told by my parents, "You can't continue high school because you have to work to help with the family's expenses." After graduating from eighth grade, she also began to work, accepting everything my parents told her. During the time we were with our family before Rosa and I got married, we gave our paycheck to my mom, no matter how much we earned. She gave us, first, 15 dollars a week. As we continued to progress in our jobs and earn more, she increased it to 20 dollars per week. Rosa bought her clothes, she would layaway clothes in stores and pay weekly until she could take them home. I, with my money, bought things for the house, rugs, towels, curtains, etc., whatever was needed, and even painted and changed lamps. I also bought underwear. Then I wore Rosa's dresses, and she wore the underwear. The day I got married, when I started packing my suitcase, I couldn't find anything to put in it, because Rosie had bought almost all the clothes!! Angel, my brother, perhaps realized that I couldn't find anything to take with me and gave me some money. I had bought the car I drove, the furniture in the house, and many other things, but when I left with Pancho after we got married, I didn't take absolutely anything.

Conchita finished what she needed to graduate from night school and took training to work in an office as an assistant, and began working in an office near the house, but she didn't like her job, as many people of very low re-sources and some were gang members there. It was not a place for such a beautiful and intelligent girl! She began to get depressed as her dream of being a nurse seemed to van-ish, and she saw no future in her job, but she had no other choice than to continue working to help the family. By then, Angel had already married, and Ricardo had gone to study at Stanford University.

CRUCIAL CHANGE FOR THE GIRLS

When Irene, whom we called Nena, was in her last year of high school, my brother Vito, who followed her, began guiding her to apply to different universities, as she wanted to continue her studies and knew that my dad wouldn't allow it. Nena didn't want to end up like the older women in the family who had to sacrifice their education to help out at home. Vito helped Nena complete applications, and when my dad's signature was needed, he signed the documents himself. Nena was accepted at Loyola Saint Mary University, a Catholic women's college. The day came when Nena had to leave because she had been accepted to live on campus. When Vito and Nena told my dad the plan, he couldn't believe it and became so angry that he told Nena, "If you go, forget you have a father and forget you have a family." Nena left crying; it must have been so hard for her, the first time she was leaving home, not knowing what awaited her in a completely unknown place, and without family support! Some of my siblings supported her, but only a little, as they were also fighting their own battles to get ahead. It was a very tough time for everyone, but they continued striving to achieve their goals. Nena was on the verge of failing her studies, but she remembered she couldn't return home defeated, and that drove her to keep trying. For a long time, she didn't come to my parents' house, and it was very sad for her. Her classmates would go home on weekends and holidays, and she would stay in the dormitories very alone. Finally, one day, she decided to return home and take the risk that my dad might send her away. She arrived very ashamed as if she had done something very wrong, but she was only doing what was fair and her right! When she arrived, my dad was in the living room reading. It was a holiday, and some of us were there. My dad looked up from his book and saw her, said nothing, and continued reading his book, but he didn't send her away, and those of us who were present welcomed her! From there, she continued visiting, and gradually, my dad began to speak to her again until the day she graduated from Saint Mary's when my dad told her, "I admire you because you were very brave. I considered you not very intelligent and did not think you were capable of graduating from a University, you have surprised me." And so she became what she wanted, a teacher of many children, as she taught for many years and was a great teacher who impacted the lives of many children and fulfilled her professional dream in what she loved so much, to become a teacher of little children!!

After Nena went to the University, my dad realized that the girls in the family also deserved the opportunity to continue their education if they wished. He allowed Concha to take some nursing classes offered at the General Hospital of Los Angeles, and that's how she achieved her lifelong goal of becoming a registered nurse. She also left home to continue her studies at college. It wasn't easy for Conchita to continue her education either; she faced many hardships and sacrifices to make her dream a reality. She graduated as a registered nurse and began working at the General Hospital of Los Angeles. She worked in various departments of the hospital and became an excellent nurse. Concha didn't settle for just being a nurse; she continued learning and educating herself and held several supervisory positions at the General Hospital of Los Angeles, eventually becoming the assistant to the general supervisor of the hospital, one of the most important positions. Concha married Nazih, who was born in Egypt, and they had Adam and Nora. Both studied university careers and have their own families.

I have a very special relationship with my sister Rosalia, who we call Rosa. She is the eldest of my sisters, and although I am almost three years older than her, we both experienced our lives in Leon, Tijuana, and California. We also married two brothers. Pancho and I married first, and three years later, Rosie married Arturo, Pancho's older brother. She moved closer to me and kept in touch with me all the time. She became my "comadre". She is the Godmother of my son Frank, and so is my brother Ricardo. Rosie is very sweet and caring. She is always willing to help, loves her brothers and sisters very much, and will do anything for all of us. Rosie and Arturo have three children, Claudia, Leticia, and Arturo Jr. She also has five grandchildren. Two beautiful girls and three handsome boys. Rosie and Arturo had a business and were very successful.

CHAPTER 8

My father had told my mother that they should not have any more children. When that happened, my mom was already pregnant. She did not tell my father. She was afraid of his reaction.

When he was told that another child was in the way, he was very angry with my mother. I confronted him for the first time, and we had a big argument.

Tere was born. She was a very sweet little girl. My mother mistreated her very much. Maybe she resented her because of the problems that she had with my father during her pregnancy.

Tere attended Santa Barbara University and became a teacher. She also had to deal with many obstacles. One of them was money. All children had the same monetary problems when they were attending school. They got scholarships and student loans. When Tere moved to Santa Barbara, Lalo was already attending the University and had a good friend named Osvaldo. Tere and He got in love. Tere became pregnant while still in school and not married. That

MAMA CHIQUITA: LITTLE MOTHER

was another traumatic experience for the brothers and sisters. Tere and Osvaldo were very brave, and even though they knew how my father was going to react, they decided to have their child. We all stood together and supported them. My father was very upset, but he had to accept that she was not the first or last unmarried pregnant girl and that it happens in good families, too. Tere and Osvaldo got married before their child was born. My father did not attend their wedding, but the rest of the family was there. Jose was born, and they had another boy, he was named Juan, like my mother's father.

Lalo, the first child born in the United States, had a very traumatic experience as a little boy. My mother worked for a while, and he and Juan, who was not going to school then, were taken to an older lady to be taken care of. She abused Lalo, and he became a very, quite sad little boy. The family had no clue what happened to Lalo. Everyone was very busy dealing with his/her own issues. Lalo was a very intelligent, handsome boy. Concha and Nena took care of him and the younger children when the older brothers and sisters left home. Lalo was the first to attend Santa Barbara University. He had a very hard time adjusting, and he had never dealt with the issues of his abuse as a little boy. In spite of all this, he became an engineer. Right after graduation, he got a very good job. Because he knew Spanish, he was sent to South America to fix enormous problems that the company was having. He had no experience as an engineer and was also a very nervous person. All of that was too much for him. He was not able to fix the problem, and he was blamed for something that he was not responsible for. That caused him another trauma.

Laura, the youngest of the girls, also went to Santa Barbara University. She is one of the prettiest of the six girls. She is tall and slender. It is amazing that she was able to attend a University, with all the stressors that it implies. She was a very nervous little girl. When she was in the Elementary School, she would vomit every day in the classroom. Rosa, the oldest, attending the same school, would go and clean up after her. How she was able to overcome her nervousness is beyond any understanding, but she did and became a prominent engineer. She worked for a company that developed new medicines. She became a supervisor at a very young age and traveled to many interesting places for conventions about new medicines. She got married to Jesus, a very good man, and they have two beautiful children. Andrea and Nico. Even though she had an excellent career, she gave it up to stay home and raise her children.

Mario is the youngest of all. He was born when I was twenty years of age. At that point, I was doing some of my father's chores. I would be the one to take my mother to the doctor's visits. My mother had had too many children (19), and she became very ill when expecting Mario. She almost lost him. In order to save him, she had to be in bed for weeks.

At that time, Rosa, the father and little mother (Picha) who was called Feli now (she never liked to be called Picha, so once the family arrived in the USA, she paid her siblings some coins every time they called her Feli, instead of Picha) were working together in an electronics company making fire alarms. My father had had an automobile accident, and since then, he never drove again. I had to learn to drive when I was 17 years old. I was a very nervous person and would suffer very much when my uncle Salvador used to take me to driving practice. My father was not able to take his responsibilities once more. He made the children do the things that he did not want to or was not able to do. They had to make phone calls for him, pay bills, etc. The children never went to him or my mother with their problems. They would have to solve them between themselves. Once, Angel had a car accident; it was his fault, so he had to pay some money to a lady. He was very worried, but he did not dare tell my parents about it. Feli came up with the money to pay the lady.

Angel married Vicky, his first love. Both were only nineteen years of age. They were both attending Northridge University. Angel and Vickie met at Guardian Angel Church. They were members of a club of young adults. In Pacoima, there were not many social events for young people, so the club was a good thing for them. Angel and Vicky have four children: Angelica, who is an excellent teacher like Tia Nena and Tia Tere. Diana, who has a degree in business and works for the Edison Electric Company, is very prominent in what she does. She is married and has two children. Rebeca is a beautiful girl who got married and has two beautiful girls and she is a very devoted mother. Miguel, the youngest one, also got a degree and lives in the Philippines, and he is the father of a little boy. So, Angel has five grandchildren whom he loves very much. Angel was a good son and an excellent brother. He loves his family very much and is always willing to help anyone who needs the help.

Juanito, the youngest of the eight children who came from Mexico, in my opinion, was the most affected by all the many changes in our lives. First of all, he was only six months of age when he was left to be taken care of by a twelve-year-old and a father who was not capable of nourishing his family. Once we came to the United States, he was told that Feli (Picha) was not his mother, that this lady that he barely knew was his mother. He was only five years old and was very attached to me, he was not able to freely come to me. Later, he shared with other siblings that even though he was in a house full of people, he felt lonely, like an orphan. To make things worse for him, he stayed with my mom for a while. I went to work, so he did not see me during the day. In Tijuana, for more than five years, he was with me every day. He was very little and could not understand what was happening. My mother also went to work and took Juanito and Lalo to an older lady who mistreated and abused them!

Juanito somehow was able to overcome much suffering. He became a handsome, good boy. Juanito is very intelligent and loves to read. He became very knowledgeable and educated. He attended the University of Santa Barbara and studied business. He was not able to finish his career. He

133

became very ill, and he developed a very severe arthritis. He had to come back home, where he was miserable. My father did not treat him well. He did not believe that Juanito was ill and that he just did not want to study or work because he was lazy. Most of the older brothers and sisters were not there anymore to support him.

Once he recuperated, he became independent. He got a good job in a bank and succeeded. He was able to travel to many countries and learn about different cultures and ways of life. All of us have had the opportunity to travel to different places, but Juanito has visited most countries.

I had been in a relationship with the love of my life for five years. Everyone thought that we were going to get married, but we surprised everyone, and after a few times of ending the relationship, we finally ended it for good. For two years, I lost interest in life. I would continue going to work, but that was about all I did.

During this time, I met Francisco (Pancho), who looked a lot like the love of my life. I believed then that I would not be able to love anybody the way I loved before, and without thinking about it, I married Pancho nine months after I met him.

That was a big mistake on my part. We married without planning for our future or anything else. I had a good, solid job, and he did not, but I moved to where he was living. At first, we were in a little furnished apartment. I became pregnant with our first child in the second month of marriage.

I had to start working at night in a very noisy, oily steel company. It was a heavy job, and I almost lost our first baby. This was not the worst thing happening. Pancho was not ready to settle down at all. He continued to party and live a life of a single person. He had a terrible temper, was very demanding, and mistreated me. He was in many ways like my father. Even though my husband was younger than me, I became afraid of him. I was not used to voicing my opinions and did not know how to defend myself.

Most of the family members thought that this marriage was not going to last. A few years passed, and I had to do something for my husband to change his ways. I decided to separate from him. We were separated for a few weeks. Pancho realized that he had a good wife, and he did not want to be separated from his three beautiful children. He came back and promised me that he was going to change. We gave our marriage a second opportunity. My husband changed completely. He was always a good worker. And a great provider. He learned to take care of his money. He became very responsible and stopped going out with his friends to party. We are still together. We have been married for almost 55 years, and I love him very much.

ACCOMPLISHMENTS

All my brothers and sisters pursued a career, except Rosie and me, as we didn't have the opportunity to be the eldest and to help with the expenses of such a large family. Vito graduated as a mechanical engineer from Stanford University the same year that Ricardo graduated as a Doctor of Medicine from the same university. Vito married Araceli, who also, once she was married, finished her education and became a caring teacher who impacted the lives of many students, especially the Spanish-speaking children, since she speaks fluent Spanish. She was also born in Mexico, and we have similar experiences. Vito an Araceli have two handsome boys, Andres and Beto, who are also very successful professionals. Ricardo married Robbie, a law student he met at Stanford University. She did not continue her studies because she had their children, Antonio, Daniel, and Armando, and dedicated herself to taking care of them while Ricardo finished his career and his medical service. Ricardo worked for Kaiser Permanente for many years. He also founded a program called the Socrates Circle to encourage low-income youth to pursue a career in medicine. He worked several years with other professionals and had the satisfaction of seeing several young people who went through his program graduate as doctors. The program was taken over by Kaiser and expanded into many other areas of California. Robbie returned to university when their children were all in school and graduated as a lawyer, a profession she practiced for several years. Antonio, their eldest son, graduated as an engineer and then returned to university and earned a second degree in law. He works at a company where he practices both his professions. Daniel, the second, dedicated himself to music and is an excellent guitarist and composer. Armando graduated in Business Administration and has a great job. The three children of Robbie and Ricardo are married, and Ricardo and Robbie have six grandchildren, three boys and three girls.

Gerardo also studied and graduated as an engineer from the University of Santa Barbara. Laura followed in the footsteps of the engineers and, despite choosing the profession of engineering, which was not very popular for a Latina girl, she succeeded and became a Chemical Engineer. She has had very good jobs in important pharmaceutical companies. Due to her work, she had to travel a lot and had two children, Andrea and Nico. After working hard for a while, she and Jesus, her husband, saved some money, and Laura retired from work to take care of their young children. Tere followed the same profession as Nena and is a very good teacher. She also achieved this with many sacrifices like the others, but like Angel, she graduated while married and with a son, Jose. For both of them, it was much more difficult to achieve their goals. Tere married Osvaldo, whom she met at the University of Santa Barbara, where they both graduated. Later, their second son, Juanito, was born. Tere's two children are also professionals. Tere has one granddaughter who was named Bella.

Gerardo's first job, whom we call Lalo, as an Engineer was in a country in South America. Almost at the end of his career, he moved to a completely strange place, surrounded by people he didn't know, and with a new job. I don't remember how long his employment lasted, but I know it didn't go well for him. I believe he never recovered from that bad experience, as he never worked as an Engineer again.

Lalo became an expert in computers, and that is what he does for a living.

Juan also attended the University of Santa Barbara. He is very intelligent but was unable to finish his degree. When the family lived in Pacoima, Juan fell ill with severe arthritis. For some reason, my father did not believe him and said that Juan was not sick, that he was lazy, and that he was inventing illnesses to avoid working or studying. Those were very tough times for Juan, as he was so afraid of my father that he would eat when everyone else was asleep. I believe Juanito was the most affected by the absence of our mother in our lives. He was just over six months old when we were left alone in Tijuana. I was in charge of his care, but how could I be a mother to him or any of my seven siblings under my care if I was only eleven years old! My father was with us, but he did not help with household chores or taking care of the children, and his sour and angry character was also no support to us. For a long time, Juanito was very ill with stomach issues, as he did not tolerate the food we gave him well. Despite everything, Juanito worked very hard for some years and then spent many more traveling the world. He is one of our family who had many experiences in different parts of the world.

Vito was always a very special child. He was born after Nena. The day he was born was late at night, almost dawn. When my mom was having her children, if it was during the day, they sent us to the park, and when we returned, they surprised us with a new baby. I had known for a long time that children weren't brought by the stork but that my mom had them. I was a very precocious child, and I noticed the changes in my mom. Besides, I was used to her having a child every year or so!! When it was night, they sent us to the kitchen, but it was so small that we lay down with our heads outside and could see the sky and the stars. And that dawn, we saw a shooting star and at that moment, we heard the baby's first cry. Later, we discovered that Vito had a swirl on the front of his head. We believed it was because of the star that fell when he was born. But truly, he was always very studious and responsible, as well as very intelligent, and he always had a lot of wisdom to support and advise his siblings, especially the youngest ones, like Mario, the youngest of all, who was nearly lost, as he was going down a very bad path with many problems. When Vito returned from the University, he decided to go back to my parents' house and help straighten out the four younger siblings who were still at home. My parents were very old and tired and had lost control of the Four Little Ones, as we called them. For my parents, it was like having another new family. The Eight, who came from Mexico, and the Four who were born in California. Mario, the youngest of the family, started to stray. He hung out with boys who were no good, and his grades were not good at all. Vito was the one who saved Mario, as he kept an eye on him and the other three young siblings. With Vito's support, Mario managed to continue his studies and became an excellent engineer, working for a long time with an oil company in a high and very responsible position. The bad thing was that he had too much stress, and his health was not good. He did not take care of himself and had a sudden heart attack and died instantly. He was only forty-eight years old. That was the great loss that our family has suffered to this day. Mario left a daughter, his beloved Maricela, and his widow Elsa. To this day, they continue to be a very important part of the life of the Sistos family. During the time that my mom lived close to us, Elsa and Maricela visited her very often. My mom had mixed feelings because, on the one hand, she was very happy to see them, and on the other, she felt great sadness because her beloved Mario did not come with them. Mario was always very close to my mom, he never stopped

141

visiting her and being very attentive to her. This loss was enormous for my mom and our whole family. Even today, we all expect to see Mario at our gatherings, with his big smile and the way he used to celebrate our family gatherings. That is why we all try to preserve our traditions, which Mario loved so much, like gathering a few days before Christmas to make tamales all together. He never missed the Tamale Day. That will be one of our traditions that we will try to keep in our family, in the name of our beloved Mario. Our children, Mario's nieces and nephews, remember him just as he was; he radiated energy, an energy of love and understanding, and we all felt very good being with him. Once, when his nieces and nephews were gathered, Frank, my son, asked, "Mario, are you here at this moment? If you are here, give us a sign." There were some lights on as everyone was outside, and the lights began to turn on and off. It was a very strong experience for everyone, as they could feel Mario's presence after his death!

Each one of us, in our own way, has achieved the American Dream. This is the country of opportunities, and if one works hard and has the vision to achieve their goals, it can be done. I, who could not continue my studies because I only went up to the middle of fifth grade in León, went back to study at night to learn English once I arrived in California. Then, I got married and had my three children, Frank, Fernando, and Alex. My husband Pancho and I worked very hard to buy our first house and to provide our children with an education. We were able to send them to private schools, as there were no good public schools in the area where we

143

lived. We were also able to pay for the universities for all three, and each of our children has a profession. Our older son Frank became a psychologist. Although he never worked in psychology, it helped him a lot to succeed in his profession. He is excellent at what he does. He is very sociable and helps whoever is in need. Our second son Fernando studied Business Administration and has worked as an accountant at a very important transport firm. He married Sandra, a beautiful girl who has been our joy, and they gave us, Pancho and me, the great joy of being grandparents to Andres, our beloved grandson. Fernando is a great son. He is our support whenever we need it; he is a good husband and a loving father. He has a very good relationship with his son. We only have one grandson, Andres, but God gave us a handsome boy with fair skin, blond hair, and big, beautiful blue eyes. Just like my parents always wanted. His eyes did not change when he turned six months of age!! He also is very athletic and loves sports and is really good at some of them. Best of all, Andres has a big heart and is a good teenage boy. We are very proud of him, and he is the light of our eyes! I know that we would have loved Andres even if he was not as handsome and as good as he is because our love for him is unconditional. For most of my existence, I felt like a disappointment to my parents for not being what they wanted me to be as their first child. It is an irony of Life that my grandson has the qualities that my father wanted me to have!

Alex studied History and Mathematics and got his Bachelor's degree. He also obtained his teaching credential. Alex was always a good student and had good grades. He graduated from High School with honors. He got a scholarship to the University he wanted to attend. His dream was to be a doctor like his uncle Ricardo. After his High School graduation, he became very ill, and it was very challenging for him to continue his studies. He attended the University for one semester, but he had to stop his career for a few years and lost his scholarship. Those years were very hard for our family. Although I had experienced many hard times throughout my whole life, the worst one was to see my very young, handsome boy very ill. He never gave up and, with great effort, managed to have a university career. Although he was not able to be a doctor, he became a teacher and a coach of High School children. We are very proud of his success because it took him years and more effort than usual to finish his education, but he got his diplomas and was able to teach young guys and girls. He now works with

145

Special Young Adults, and his own hardships help him become an excellent person, willing to help whoever is in need.

I was also able to continue my education once my children went to school all day. I started by working to obtain my high school diploma at a school for adults. Later, I worked at a school, taking care of children in the playground. After that, I took classes to become a Teacher's Assistant, and I worked as a teacher's assistant for some time. I was never able to become a children's teacher because I couldn't dedicate all my time to studying; I had to work, and at that time, we were paying for our three children's education. They were very close in age, and all three were in university almost at the same time. I continued applying for new positions in the Montebello School District until I reached the Office of the Head Start Program and worked several years as a Parent Educator, which was a very good job for me. I did not become a children's teacher, but I always worked in schools in the area of education. To advance in my position, I continued taking classes in Social Studies and Child Psychology. I had the satisfaction of taking many university courses in the classroom; I always felt like a fish in water! I had many satisfactions in my profession, as I had the opportunity to work with children and families with limited resources. I was able to help many families improve their way of life through parent education and resources to get ahead. I retired from the job I loved so much at 64 years old.

For five years after my retirement, I had the beautiful experience of taking care of my beloved grandson, Andres. For me, it was a very beautiful experience to be able to care for and enjoy him with all the time in the world. This helped me make peace with myself for not having been able to give my three children the time and care they needed when they were little. For many years, the guilt of not being able to take care of my boys the way I should have hunted me, and I felt that I was not a good mother because I was too busy, although I tried to give them quality time by singing with them when they took a bath and put them to sleep. I remember that when Frank and Fernando were very young, I taught them a Spanish song, and they formed a duet and sang the whole song beautifully!! I finally made peace with myself. I know that I did what I needed to do to try to give my children a better life than mine.

My father died in 2004. His plan upon coming to California was to stay here for about five years, save some money, and return to our homeland, León Guanajuato. However, he ended up staying in the Mission of San Fernando. My father was very proud to be Mexican; he loved his country dearly and taught us to love it as well. He was also grateful to the United States of America for the great opportunities his children received, enabling us to get a good education and a much better standard of living than we could have had if we had stayed in our country of origin.

Most of our children have university educations and are also achieving their goals. They all know that dreams can be fulfilled; you just have to study and work hard. They have the example of our family of immigrants, who arrived in this country without money, being a large family, but with a hunger to get ahead and succeed, even though it seemed very difficult and nearly impossible to achieve those dreams.

After my father's death, my mother sold the little house we bought in Pacoima when we arrived in the United States and bought a nice, comfortable condominium where she lived her last years. My mother lived very close to me for a little more than fifteen years. We attended to all her needs and can say with satisfaction that she lived her last days comfortably and contentedly in her own home. In her last two years, my mother lost almost all her physical mobility, but mentally, she was very lucid and alert. Living close to my mother in the last years of her life gave me the opportunity to get to know her better and learn to love her for who she was—a woman who suffered a lot, very strong and determined.

It was because of my mother's vision that our large family is in this country. She, who could not have the education to which she was entitled, though she was very intelligent, achieved a great change through her tenacity and vision— the improvement of a humble and poor family that, through

149

many sacrifices and hard work, achieved the American Dream.

Pancho and I have only one grandson, Andres, son of Fernando, and my beautiful Sandra. I hope that Andres will continue our legacy of improvement, as that is what all of us want, a better life for all the descendants of the family, who one day, our parents, Ricardo Sistos Barreto and Irene De La Cruz Hernandez, decided to leave their land and embark on a journey without knowing the outcomes or risks that would occur. They had in mind to improve the possibilities for their family. We can affirm that their dream was fulfilled, and we must be thankful for everything the family has been able to achieve.

My greatest satisfaction is my sons Francisco Jr (Panchito), Fernando, and Alex. All three have a university education. I am satisfied that with my husband Francisco (Pancho), we were able to support our children in achieving their goals.

As I said, we only have one grandson, Andres. Rosa and Arturo have five; Claudia's are Diego and Elianna. Leti's are Jordan, Tyler, and Conner. Angel and Victoria have four; Rebeca's are Monet and Zoey; Diana's are Daniel and Sophia. Ricardo and Roberta have six; Antonio's are Rafael and Karina; Daniel's are Daniela and Julie; Armando's are Cruz and Leonardo. Concha and Nazih have four; Adam's are Luca and Jacob; Nora's are Amelia and Atticus. Tere and Osvaldo have one; Jose's is named Belle. They are all a new generation of the Sistos in the United States of America, the land of opportunities. In this country, if one works hard with a goal in mind, one can make their dreams realities.

LETTERS

ROSAS STORY (ROSALIA)

My name is Rosalia, and I am the second oldest in the family. What I remember about Leon Guanajuato is when my dad was not home on Saturdays at night, my mom would tell us stories. I enjoyed them very much because she made me use my imagination. When my parents decided to come to Tijuana to try to reach the United States looking for a better future, we traveled by train. We were ten of us including my parents. There was little space, and we slept on the floor between the seats.

When we arrived in Tijuana a few months later, my mother went to the United States to work with the purpose of bringing us to this country. We stayed with my dad. He oversaw cooking and making flour tortillas for us. My sister Feli, who was only 12 years old, took care of all of us, ages 6 months to 10 years old. I remember that the hardest job for her was washing our clothes by hand. It was an incredibly sad time to be without my mother.

After 5 years, my mother arranged our documents, and we were all happy because we were finally going to be together. We arrived in the city of Pacoima, California, and they immediately enrolled us in a Catholic school. We got a good deal because the maximum tuition they charged was for three students, and there were six of us. The first day before entering the classroom, we said the pledge of allegiance, and it made me cry because I was missing my country. We did not know English, so they sent me and my brothers Angel and Ricardo to the same classroom in fifth grade. At the end of sixth grade, we were moved to eighth grade, and we were able to graduate. My brothers were able to continue studying. I was about to turn sixteen, so I had to start working to help my parents. By then, Gerardo and Teresa had already been born. Years later Laura and Mario came.

In 1972, I married Arturo, a responsible and diligent man. I only worked for 5 years because he was able to buy a gas station, and I was able to stay home to take care of my three children. Claudia is a teacher at an elementary school, and her children are Diego and Eliana. Her husband is George. Leticia is a registered nurse and has a doctorate. She works for Riverside County and is also a professor at a university. Her children are Jordan, Tyler, and Connor. Her husband is Joshua. All my grandchildren are doing very well in school. Arturo Jr. is a responsible and diligent man as well as his father.

I am enormously proud of my siblings for being the first generation to obtain a university degree. It was not easy. With a lot of effort and sacrifice, they managed to overcome all the challenges to achieve their dreams. I think my family did very well. Out of twelve siblings, eleven were able to go to university. When I was 50 years old, I was able to obtain my GED.

ANGEL'S STORY

My name is Angel the third eldest and first boy in a family of 12 children. I was named after my paternal grandfather and my Dad's older brother. My earliest memories are somewhat vague. One of them occurred when I was 3 or 4 years old; I remember falling into a tub of water and a man pulling me out. At the time, I believe we were living in a place adjacent to the small shoe factory where our Dad worked in Leon, Guanajuato. The man that pulled me out might have been a coworker of my Dad.

Another memory is a time when I was maybe 5 years old. I recall having a severe case of dizziness and nausea, so severe that I couldn't even move my head without feeling horrible. On that occasion, after a few awful days, my mother wrapped me in her shawl and took me to see a doctor. The delay in seeing a doctor may have been because she didn't have the money right away. I think this condition may have been vertigo caused by an ear infection. I am not sure if this condition had any effect on my overall hearing, but as a small child, I recall hearing people talk on the radio and not understanding a word they were saying. It was like in the Charlie Brown cartoons when adults speak, all you hear is muffled mumbles. To this day, I have trouble under-standing conversations, especially in crowded places.

Some memories are sad and funny. I recall one night waking up at night and being alone with my younger brother Ricardo. Apparently my mother had left with our two older sisters to attend a Posada (Xmas celebration). My mother had left a kerosene lamp on. Ricardo and I were scared to be alone. I had the idea to turn off the lamp so that daylight would come sooner; my rationale was that every time I went to sleep, I would soon wake up to daylight. After a few minutes in darkness, we were even more scared and couldn't turn on the lamp because we couldn't find the matches. Luckily, soon after, our mother returned to find us both crying.

When I was seven years old, in 1957, we moved to Ti-juana with the hope that soon we would be able to immi-grate to the US. Expecting to immigrate quickly, our par-ents did not enroll us in school for several months. It turned out that it was more difficult to immigrate than our parents anticipated. We ended up living in Tijuana for 5 years. Our mother was able to enter the US right away since she had been born in California. She left us with our dad for almost the entire 5 year period. Those years were difficult but very formative. I think it stilled in us a hunger for a better life and the desire to excel in order to realize our dreams.

I remember spending long periods of time alone, in a vacant hill behind the one room shack where we lived. I often daydreamed about becoming something like an engineer or builder and transforming the poverty-stricken neighborhood into a little paradise with beautiful homes, roads, bridges, and gardens. Most of the homes in our neighborhood were built with tar paper or cardboard, or whatever materials were easily available. This was perhaps the beginning of my dream of becoming an engineer or something similar. Most of us did very well in school in Tijuana. Unfortunately, Feli, being the oldest, was not enrolled in school because she had to take care of the youngest of our siblings. It was indeed unfortunate because she probably liked school more than any one of us and would have done great in whatever career she had chosen.

Finally, in 1962, we were granted US citizenship through naturalization from our mother. We were fortunate that most of us, except Feli and the two youngest brothers, were admitted to Guardian Angel Catholic School. Since

MAMA CHIQUITA: LITTLE MOTHER

Feli was already about 16 years old, she immediately started to work to help support the family.

During that period, I had a very close relationship with two of my younger brothers, Victorio and Juan. I recall spending time with them, telling them made-up stories about wild animals doing heroic things. Like the story of a cub lion that was captured by hunters but later managed to escape and return to Africa. Nowadays, I also like to tell stories to my grandchildren about heroic animals or little children doing amazing things. After graduating from Guardian Angel in the 8th grade, I was almost 15 years old, despite the fact that Rosa, Ricardo, and I skipped the 7th grade. Most kids graduating from Guardian Angel would go on to Catholic high school. However, with me, it was different. From very early on, I always felt that I was a burden on my parents. Going to a Catholic high school entailed paying expensive tuition, which would have burdened my parents further. Therefore, I decided to go to San Fernando High School, a public school in the City of San Fernando. I faced a lot of opposition from my parents and even the parish priest. They all told me that I would become a juvenile delinquent. Nevertheless, I was determined to go to public high school and prove them wrong. I managed to convince the counselor at San Fernando High to allow me to skip the 9th grade and go directly to the 10th grade.

For a large portion of my high school days, I was an extremely shy, introverted person with no friends. I seldom spoke in the classroom. Not until about the 11th grade did I manage to make friends. Fernando Briones and Robert Ineriz were the ones who approached me one day while we were playing basketball during gym class. They had been friends since the first grade. They both played an important role in my life.

Throughout high school, I maintained very good grades, about a 3.5 grade point average. In fact, my grades were all A's and B's, never even a "C." Despite this, my immediate goal upon graduation was to get a job and help support the family. It was not until I was in the 12th grade, just a couple months prior to graduation, did I started to consider the possibility of going to college. This possibility was mostly because of the insistence of Fernando and Robert.

One day, some students from San Fernando Valley State College (now called California State University at Northridge, CSUN) visited my school. They informed us that the college had just started a special program for minority students called the Student Assistance Program (SAP).

They convinced me to apply despite the fact that I had not taken the SAT. I often think now that if I had been absent that day, I would not have found out about the SAP and, most likely, would have ended up being drafted to fight in the Vietnam War. Our counselors at San Fernando High were not very proactive and encouraging; I don't recall ever discussing with them the possibility of going to college. In September 1968, I started attending college, majoring in engineering. I believe I was the first on both sides of the family to ever go to college. College was not easy for me. Since I had to support myself and did not have a scholarship, I had to work part-time while taking a full load of classes. I also had not developed good studying habits or time management skills. In class I would often feel tired and sleepy and would miss much of the lecture. My method to catch up was to study on my own and engage in all-nighters to prepare just prior to exams. Thankfully, a professor by the name of Ray Landis became my advisor and helped to develop better studying habits and improve my performance in class.

In the summer of 1969, I met my future wife, Vicky. I had seen her a couple years before in high school. The first time I saw her, I was in an auto mechanics class, facing the hallway. I saw this very pretty, slender girl pass by, wearing very plain clothes and no makeup at all. After that instance, I saw her only a few more times in passing but did not speak to her.

During summer break in 1969, Ricardo and I became members of the Catholic Youth Organization (CYO) at Guardian Angel Catholic Church. It was at that time that I saw Vicky again since she and her younger sister, Mina, were also CYO members. Vicky and I became friends and went on several excursions with the rest of the club members. It was a very enjoyable time; the CYO was a great way to meet decent girls. Several CYO members developed romantic relationships, which ended in marriage.

In the spring of 1970, Vicky graduated from high school. I encouraged her to apply to go to college despite the fact that she had not taken any college preparatory courses.

Most of her classes had been to prepare her to become a secretary or office worker. She was accepted into CSUN through SAP. In college, we often got together to study or go to lunch. Due to her lack of preparation, she really had a hard time in college. Most of the classes she took were remedial courses.

Around the middle of 1970, our friendship developed into something more serious, and we became romantically involved. Later that year, we both decided to move into college dormitories. Our relationship became more involved. One thing led to another, and in early 1971, Vicky became pregnant. I think I was in love with her and could not accept leaving her or our future child. We decided to marry, against the advice of everyone in my family, our parish priest, and my college advisor, Professor Landis. On April 16, 2071, we married in a very humble ceremony at the Santa Rosa Catholic Church in San Fernando. Vicky was a couple months pregnant but was still very slender. She looked radiant and beautiful. My parents did not attend my wedding, but all my brothers and sisters did.

My father was very upset with me. He told me that I would not be able to graduate from college in light of the responsibilities of marriage. He believed that I would set a bad precedent for my younger brothers and sisters. However, I never doubted my commitment to graduating as an engineer and decided to prove him wrong. In hindsight, I think he was using reverse psychology to give me the necessary incentive to finish my studies.

Since we did not receive any public assistance, Vicky dropped out of college and started to work soon after our first daughter was born. I also worked during summer breaks and part-time while attending school. It was a very difficult time; we barely had enough to pay rent and pay for tuition and books. I remember one time when I ran out of gasoline and had to push my old 56 Chevy over a street block to the nearest gas station. At the gas station, I put in $2 worth of gas and attempted to pay with a bag of pennies. The attendant refused to take my payment. Luckily, a young man around my age gave me $2 dollar bills in exchange for my bag of pennies.

Being married with a child and going to college full-time was very difficult. We did not have the money nor the time for Vicky and I to go out to enjoy an evening together, since I had to study most of the time. On weekends, we would go to the college gardens to enjoy the weather while I studied and our daughter Angelica played on the grass.

Finally, in the spring of 1973, I graduated from college with a degree in Mechanical Engineering. Again, I believe I was the very first in several generations on both sides of the family to graduate from college. Our lives started to improve. I was fortunate to be hired by the Southern California Edison (SCE) Company as an Associate Engineer. I soon started working on the San Onofre Nuclear Generation Station (SONGS) Project, daring the start of construction. I worked through the completion of construction, startup, and operation for almost 40 years. I was promoted several times, becoming supervisor of a team of engineers and designers. I finally decided to retire in November 2012 at the age of 63. Working for SCE was the best professional decision that I made in my career. It gave me financial independence, and I was able to provide for my children's material needs. Unfortunately, I cannot say the same thing about providing for their emotional needs. But that is another story.

CONCHA'S STORY

This is Concha, one of the six Sistos sisters. I am writing this segment of my life regarding the educational endeavor I went through. I trust it could reveal some valuable measures to a difficult period of my life that few of my siblings might have been aware of.

To start off, it should be stated that our parents made a financial sacrifice to have all of us start on the right educational path by attending a catholic private school up until the 8th grade. Providing us with a good, sound early education was a priority for my father. He wasn't aware that some of us had goals to continue a higher level of education.

Everything was going as planned for me until the beginning of my senior year of high school. Rosa, my older sister, was engaged to be married, and since I was the next older daughter, my father demanded that I quit school and start working to help provide for the family. My high school counselor, being aware of my situation, made some arrangements to help me. In addition to the day classes, before the semester ended, he arranged for me to attend night school

166

classes to take two additional classes a semester. It turned out I had the grades and enough units to obtain my high school diploma.

Unfortunately, my dream of going to college was shattered, and I ended up leaving school by the end of the first semester. Reluctantly, I began working in a nearby electronic factory that enabled me to provide the family with the needed financial assistance. The following year, my younger sister Nena, secretly and without my parents' consent, applied to a private all-girls university and was accepted. Even after she left, I felt an obligation to stay home and continue to help and provide.

During that stage of my life, I felt that my future did not hold a bright, promising way of life for me, and I would be categorized as the 'Old Maid' living at home for the rest of my existence. My life totally collapsed after I failed the State Boards' examination for a license in vocational nursing, which I had completed a program at an occupational center for. I was devastated and desperately wanted someone to come to my rescue, so I faked an attempted suicide, taking aspirin with a bottle of wine to alert my parents. I made sure someone knew my plan and told my younger sister Tere what I was doing. I still remember my father coming to my room and sitting next to me while I was still holding the bottle of wine and a few aspirins. Totally out of character, he calmly told me that I had so much potential and that he knew that I could accomplish anything I wanted. He told me I no longer needed to provide money for the family and that my only responsibility was to seek and pursue my dreams.

Finally, at 21 years old, I reapplied to a nursing program and was accepted; two years later, I obtained a license as a registered nurse. Many years later, after marriage and having two children, I decided to realize my educational goal, attended Cal State Los Angeles, and obtained a BS in Nursing.

Reflecting on this ordeal, I realize that my parents had an immense financial responsibility with twelve children. In our father's mind, it was culturally acceptable to demand that his older daughters (Feli, Rosa, and I) work to help support the family. He was confident that each one of us would eventually find a husband to support us. I do not resent or hold any ill feelings toward him. I know he was doing what he thought was in the best interest of the whole family.

NENA'S STORY

My worst memory of my childhood was ironically, the reunification of our family. Our mother had been away from us for five years, residing in the US while we remained in Tijuana. She was the main provider for the family. Although our father remained with us in Tijuana, he was incapable of taking care of us due to his excessive drinking. At times, he would be gone for days only to return to us drunk or hung over.

Once we were all able to migrate to the US, our household was filled with tension and frustration. It was not an easy transition or adjustment for any of us. Our parents lacked the maturity and understanding to give us the love and attention we desired. Faced with the burden of financial responsibility for children that they had no emotional attachment to their frustration led them to inappropriate behavior. In addition to our father being an alcoholic, he would have frequent episodes of rage. We went out of our way to avoid him due to his volatile temper. Our mother displayed her anger and frustration by using some of us as scapegoats. Unfortunately, I was one of them. I don't care

169

to elaborate on her treatment of me since I've chosen to put it behind me. Needless to say, it was a miserable existence. Personally, I longed for the years in Tijuana (away from my parents), where I had the freedom to run and roam wildly through the hills near our modest home.

During that time, my strongest desire was to run away from it all. I realized that the only way out was to go to college. I had never considered myself college material because I believed I wasn't smart enough. Indirectly, I felt compared to my younger brother Vito, who was extremely gifted, and also to my older sister Concha, who was both pretty and smart. I couldn't possibly compete with either of them. However, my desire to get away was stronger than my insecurities. With the help and guidance of my older brothers, I applied to a few colleges. To my surprise, I was accepted to all of them and was even offered a few scholarships. The rest would be provided by the work/study program at the college. I chose to go to Mount St. Mary's College (MSMC) because my best friend Sylvia wanted to go there due to its excellent nursing program. Unfortunately, she didn't get accepted. I decided to go anyway, thinking that my parents would approve of it since it was a Catholic, all-women's college.

I still recall feeling terrified and apprehensive about my decision to leave home. I didn't bother to share my plans with my parents for fear of their reaction. My brother Vito helped me forge my father's signature in all my applications. I waited a week before leaving to break the news to my parents. Their reaction was less than encouraging. My father warned me that if I left, I would not be welcomed back. He didn't believe women needed a college education since we were expected to get married and be supported by our husbands. In spite of this, I left feeling miserable and scared. I had made my decision, and I was not going to back down.

My first year in school was miserable. I realized how ill-prepared I was for college. Many of the girls who attended MSMC, came from wealthy families and had gone to the best prep schools in the country. I was an English learner, socially inadequate and with a very poor high school education. I purposely skipped orientation week because I was afraid of not fitting in. I was right. Immediately, I felt like an outsider. I had nothing in common with these girls. By the time I arrived at the Mount, most of them had formed friendships and cliques.

I often sat alone in the dining room because I lacked the social skills to make new friends. I felt completely inadequate and alone. I struggled academically and socially. However, I felt I had no other option but to endure these difficult times. Going back home was not an option!

After several weeks of loneliness and misery, one of my classmates took a liking to me. Her name was Celia, and she was a Cuban refugee. The only thing we had in common was that we both spoke Spanish and we were both immigrants. Her family had been wealthy in Cuba. However, they lost everything when Fidel Castro came into power. She was friendly and outgoing and introduced me to her friends. Celia and her friends were a few years older and lived off-campus. At least I was less lonely during the day.

I struggled for two years at MSMC, but I managed to improve my grades enough to transfer to Loyola Marymount University. My experiences at Loyola were drastically different from that of MSMC. At Loyola, I was able to thrive socially and academically. I graduated with a Bachelor of Arts degree and later obtained a Credential from Cal State LA.

I don't regret my decision to leave home because this experience made me a stronger person. I finally was able to recognize in myself abilities I didn't know I had.

VITO'S STORY (VICTORIO)

My earliest childhood memories are of when I was about five years old in Tijuana, where my siblings, four sisters, three brothers, and my father lived. My mother, who was working in the US to support the family, would visit us occasionally, so my memories of her during that time are vague. I remember home being a small, one-room shack with no plumbing. I don't recall any furniture, only a pile of old coats that my older sisters would spread out on the floor and we would use as bedding. Home was situated close to a dirt road, so I remember waking up mornings covered in the dust raised by the buses and cars that rumbled by throughout the night. On some occasions, it would be so bad that my eyes would be caked over, and my older sisters would have to wipe them clean with a wet rag before I could open them. Life during that period was, to me, an adventure. When my older siblings went off to school, I was pretty much left to my own devices. After wolfing down a breakfast typically of beans and flour tortillas, I would venture off into the nearby hills. These hills which were typically barren and dusty, were for me a place of exploration. But they would transform into lush grasslands during the wet season. I remember roaming through chest-high grass, making my way to the highest hilltop. There, I would gaze down on my ramshackle barrio, searching for the shack I called home, knowing that I would make my way back when I got hungry.

Life changed dramatically when we left Tijuana to live in the US. It was necessary to split us up into two or three vehicles in order that we all could fit. I recall making the trip with several of my siblings in a big black sedan owned by a family relative already living in the US. On the way, our driver decided to take a route along the San Diego waterfront. Never had I seen anything like what I saw that day. There were enormous Navy vessels with their massive gray steel hulls looming in the distance. All around were tall buildings with windows like mirrors reflecting the sunlight down onto clean, paved streets. I marveled at the wide highway filled with what looked to me like brand-new cars, and off in the distance were beautiful homes with green, grass-covered yards. We arrived at the home of my father's niece later that day, where several of us were to stay for a while. It was immaculate with carpeted and tiled floors, decorated with beautiful furniture and best of all, indoor plumbing. I was six years old, and it was then that I realized we were poor.

After a while, the family moved into a small rental in the city of Pacoima in the San Fernando Valley. The memories I have during that period are primarily of going to Guardian Angel Catholic School and navigating a foreign culture and language. Thankfully, the teachers were bilingual nuns, and Mother Rose, my first-grade teacher, would keep me after school every day to teach me English, which I quickly learned. A year or two later, my parents bought a small house on Hoyt Street in Pacoima. While small, the house had three bedrooms and one-and-half baths, which I would share with my parents and, by now, 11 siblings, six sisters and five brothers. There was a room for my parents, a girl's room, and a boy's room, each with two bunk beds and not much more, that six each would share. This was to become the permanent family home.

Times were difficult during this period. I was a very insecure and shy kid, which was only aggravated by my father's insistence that we excel at everything. I remember bringing home a report card with all A's, with the exception of one B and my father reprimanding me for not getting straight A's. Naturally after that, straight A's is what I got.

But even then, my father would just glance at my report card and grunt his approval, rarely giving me a word of praise or encouragement. Nonetheless, I found some comfort in schoolwork and would challenge myself to be the best academically I could possibly be. Growing up in such a large family, one does not get much attention. Both my mother and father, as well as my older sisters, were focused on working to provide for the family, leaving little time for anything else. I recall one year on my 10th or 11th birthday, no one remembered it. It was later that evening that finally my oldest sister remembered and rushed out to get me a gift. In summer, I would give myself projects to keep busy. One such project was building a go-cart, just like I'd seen built by some kids on TV. I recall going off on my own to scavenge along the railroad tracks and back alleys for needed materials. I spent days collecting what I thought I'd need and then having to improvise for not having the proper tools for the project. But it was vision and determination that drove me regardless of the obstacles. I learned to visualize what it was that I wanted and then systematically develop the plan to achieve the objective. While the lack of resources made the successful execution of those plans a rarity, this thought process became a foundational element in my life.

My teenage years were perhaps the most difficult of all. I obtained my driver's license at the age of 15 because of necessity. My father was always extremely nervous about driving, and because my older siblings were either already married or busy with school and part-time work, I became the family chauffeur. This meant that I would have to drive my parents to work every morning before school and be there and waiting at precisely 4:30 pm to pick them up. Naturally, maintenance of the family vehicle also became my responsibility. I recall when I was 16 or so, having to take the car in for repairs. Naturally, I had no idea what I was doing, and I'm sure the mechanic took advantage of that. But worse yet was my father's irate disapproval of how I had allowed that to happen. Weekends, too, were difficult because that is when my father would go out to drink. I recall many Saturday nights when my father would come home intoxicated and in a foul mood, ready to berate whom-ever he encountered. In one instance, he had had an argu-ment with the bartender and was in a particularly aggra-vated state, insisting on taking a butcher knife to teach the guy a lesson. I recall standing in his way to keep him from leaving and trying to reason with him for what seemed like hours to diffuse the situation.

Things changed dramatically when I was 17. Academically, I had excelled and with the help of several caring high school teachers, I applied and was accepted to Stanford University. Never having been away from home, the 10-hour bus ride there on my own was a very intimidating event, but it also marked a transition to an entirely new life. Ironically, it wasn't until I lived in the college dorm that, for the first time ever, I had a bed all to myself. In fact, it was in college that I recognized that my life was full of potential. What I visualized then more than anything else was to someday have a place of my own, and college provided me with the resources to achieve that objective. Living away from home also gave me a new perspective on life. I now knew that my home situation was temporary, which was very helpful, especially when I returned home during school breaks and summers. I recall coming home during those breaks only to find the house in desperate need of repairs. During those times at home, it became a self-appointed job to fix whatever was amiss: broken washing machine, leaky plumbing, faulty heater, and one summer, re-shingle the leaky roof.

After graduating from college with an engineering degree and having found an engineering position near home, I decided not to rent an apartment but instead move back home for a while because part of the plan was to save for a house. During that period both my father and mother had mellowed out quite a bit. This lax attitude, unfortunately had a negative effect on my younger brothers and sisters still living at home. They had become quite rebellious, with little regard for rules or academics. Realizing that intervention was needed, I took on the paternal role and proceeded for the next couple of years to realign and focus them on their academic future. It was difficult, but in the end, they came around. Also, during this period, I grew closer to my mother. I would contribute to the household financially, and she would fix my meals, do my laundry, and iron, but more importantly, my mother made time to talk to me. I remember having many long conversations about her childhood and the challenges she endured growing up. I came to appreciate that she had to overcome many obstacles, some very harsh, to make a better life for herself and her children.

Soon thereafter, I was able to save enough and, with the help of my oldest brother, buy my first home. I finally had a place I could call my own. That was the fruition of a vision for a better life that began in the mind of a 6-year-old boy and remained in me to this day.

LAURA'S STORY

Growing up as one of twelve children in a family with parents with limited academic experience and who provided limited support for a higher education, my journey to success was fraught with numerous obstacles and challenges. Yet, it is through these very challenges that I found the resilience and determination to forge my own path.

The atmosphere at home was often tense and unpredictable due to my father's temper. This environment instilled a deep-seated fear and insecurity in me, affecting my ability to stand up for myself and seek help. My father's outbursts and the constant need to monitor his mood contributed significantly to my low self-esteem and lack of confidence. However, my older siblings played a crucial role in my development. My brother Vito, in particular, became a mentor, helping me with math and science and encouraging me to apply for college and financial aid.

Some of my earliest memories revolve around the anxiety and fear I felt about going to school. Living a sheltered life, the sudden exposure to a world outside my home was overwhelming. My parents, though providing basic necessities, failed to nurture my confidence or prepare me for the world beyond our household. They were more concerned with avoiding embarrassments, such as ending up pregnant as a teenager or becoming involved with gangs or drugs than encouraging academic or personal growth.

High school was a turning point for me. Enrolling in a College Preparation Magnet program, I found guidance and support from my teachers and older siblings. While my parents remained indifferent, my siblings' mentorship and their own academic successes became a beacon of hope, helping me navigate the complexities of preparing for college.

My father's discouragement echoed in my mind as I entered college. He believed I wasn't cut out for higher education, a sentiment that compounded my already low self-esteem and imposter syndrome. Despite these internal battles, I persevered, even surviving academic probation through sheer determination and the guidance of a compassionate College of Engineering Dean.

The real turning point came when I enrolled in Dr. Agrawal's Biomedical Engineering course. This decision was driven by a desire to prove myself capable and to pursue a meaningful career. My initial encounter with Dr. Agrawal was during his introductory Chemical Engineering course, where I went to his office hours seeking help. Dr. Agrawal pointed out that excelling in my studies required learning from my mistakes, practicing until I understood my errors, and developing a disciplined study routine. At the time, his criticism felt too similar to the discouragement I often received from my father, leaving me in tears.

However, I later realized that Dr. Agrawal's words were not meant to discourage me but to provide constructive guidance on how to succeed. When I decided to take his Biomedical Engineering course, I was determined to show both him and myself that I could thrive. I immersed myself in the course material, applying his advice, and not only excelled academically but also reignited my passion for Chemical Engineering. Dr. Agrawal remembered our previous interaction and recommended me for a summer internship at Amgen, a then-new biotechnology start-up. This opportunity became the foundation of my successful career in biotechnology and other highly regulated industries.

Reflecting on my journey, I realize that success is rarely achieved in isolation. It was the love and support from my siblings, teachers, and mentors that enabled me to overcome my challenges. Ultimately, my success was a blend of their support and my own resilience and determination. Through these experiences, I have learned that believing in oneself and seeking support are key ingredients to overcoming any obstacle.

www.ingramcontent.com/pod-product-compliance
Lightning Source LLC
Chambersburg PA
CBHW051152120626
46547CB00012B/1056